A Bit of Velvet and a Dash of Lace

THE FABULOUS INTERIORS OF MAGNOLIA PEARL

COUNTRY LIVING

A Bit of Velvet and a Dash of Lace

THE FABULOUS INTERIORS OF MAGNOLIA PEARL

ROBIN BROWN WITH JASON BOYD

PHOTOGRAPHY BY STEVEN RANDAZZO

HEARST BOOKS

A division of Sterling Publishing Co., Inc.

New York / London

www.sterlingpublishing.com

Produced by Jennifer Vreeland
Book design by Jon Zabala

Library of Congress Cataloging-in-Publication Data available.

10 9 8 7 6 5 4 3 2 1

Published by Hearst Books
A Division of Sterling Publishing Co., Inc.
387 Park Avenue South, New York, NY 10016

Country Living and Hearst Books are trademarks of
Hearst Communications, Inc.

www.countryliving.com

For information about custom editions, special sales, premium and corporate purchases, please contact Sterling Special Sales Department at 800-805-5489 or specialsales@sterlingpublishing.com.

Distributed in Canada by Sterling Publishing
c/o Canadian Manda Group, 165 Dufferin Street
Toronto, Ontario, Canada M6K 3H6

Distributed in Australia by Capricorn Link (Australia) Pty. Ltd.
P.O. Box 704, Windsor, NSW 2756 Australia

Manufactured in China

Sterling ISBN 978-1-58816-578-7

www.sterlingpublishing.com

I'd like to dedicate this book to God for inviting me to his amazing art opening; my parents, Preston and Anna, who were the two most creative people I have ever known; and my partner, John Gray, for giving me the wings to fly this dream.

Acknowledgments

Special thanks go to my co-author, Jason Boyd, and writer/editor, Brooke Maples Kotfas; our family, Preston Gray, Florence Suttle, Thovas and Tina Brown, Dan and Ballan Keen, Robert, Kathleen, Clara, and Chloe Keen, and Helen Norris; the folks at Country Living *including Nancy Soriano and Jennifer Vreeland; photographer Steven Randazzo; the staff of Sterling Publishing and Hearst Books, especially Marisa Bulzone and Jacqueline Deval; our business associates at HEB Central Market and Marburger Farm Antique Show; and all of our friends who are the "helping hands" of Magnolia Pearl such as Todd Hallmark, Dixie and Robert Cohn, Pam Heinen, LuAnn and Kenny Wayne Carter, Gail Denkhaus, Jorge and Maricella Comacho, Elizabeth and Gary Fagan, Binky Morgan, Ron Anderson, Christina Blackledge, John Sauls, Jill Elliott, Kristin Hansen, Beth Woodson, Cindy and Jason Segrest, Carol and Tim Bolton, and Traci Goudie.*

Finally, I wish to convey my sincere appreciation and gratitude to all the loving and faithful supporters of Magnolia Pearl.

—Robin

Contents

Foreword

BY NANCY SORIANO

I first discovered Magnolia Pearl at the Marburger Farm Antique Show in 2002 and immediately became excited about the idea of featuring Robin "Pearl" Brown and her husband John Gray's home in Country Living. *By that time she was already becoming a favorite designer. Women were snapping up her vintage bags and clothing; all combining antique lace, tapestry, silks, and velvets. Her one-of-a-kind approach to home decoration sets her apart as she combines rich colors, textures, and materials into works of art, not merely articles of clothing or furniture. When I met her, I knew she had a fascinating story to tell. Her layered interiors are an eclectic mix of Victorian, Oriental, and vintage American décor, filled with the antique fabrics and embroidered linens she loves. Robin's designs and home have now been featured in* Country Living *several times and our readers love reading*

about them. She exemplifies an entrepreneurial spirit, someone whose personal style

and vision has been the energy behind her successful business. This book will take

you on a wonderful journey, layer through layer, through the childhood, inspirations,

and home of the remarkable woman behind Magnolia Pearl. I hope by the end of

the following pages that you are inspired to go hunt for treasures, and perhaps add

some touches of bohemian chic to your own life (I know I have). I know you'll be as

intrigued and delighted by Robin Brown as I still am today.

–Nancy Mernit Soriano

Editor in Chief, Country Living

Preface

LIVE THE LIFE YOU LOVE

I have had the pleasure of being one of Robin's best friends for ten years and I have watched her artistic style blossom into what it is today. It's not often that most of us get a glimpse into the mind of an artist, get to hear her stories and insights firsthand—and Robin's stories always leave you feeling good. I can assure you that her outlook on life and love, art and beauty has enriched my life. It can do the same for you. I hope that after reading this book, you will feel that you know Robin, because that's the key to truly understanding Magnolia Pearl.

One more note: Like so many gifted artists, Robin is humble and down-to-earth, and she doesn't give herself the credit she deserves. (That's where I come in.) She lavishes praise on those who have influenced her and feels grateful that she's been allowed the opportunity to do what she loves for a living. It's reflective of what she believes: Live the life you love, trust in your beliefs . . . and don't take it all too seriously.

—Jason Boyd

Robin Brown, on her porch in Bandera, Texas.

ROBIN BROWN

A Flower Child Blooms

THE HEART IS THE BOSS...LOVE IT!

Robin as a young child.

OPPOSITE: Magnolia Pearl Couture fashion and backpack.

HAVE YOU EVER SEEN JERRY GARCIA NAKED? I have. What has that got to do with decorating, you ask? Well, nothing—but it might help you understand where I come from. That was just one of many experiences I had as a child growing up in California during the psychedelic 1960s. The people and events of those times colored my mind like a Technicolor trip on a bus full of Merry Pranksters headed to a Jefferson Airplane concert.

Jerry Garcia lived a few houses down from us in Hollywood when I was five, and he had a habit of gardening in the nude. But since most people in my neighborhood did that, it wasn't exactly a big deal. I wasn't embarrassed—at the time, those were the sights you encountered when you went out for a bike ride.

So I just kept on truckin'.

People always ask what my inspirations are for my decorations and designs. The short answer is, simply, poverty and imagination. One might say that I was born with a tarnished vintage silver spoon in my mouth. I come from a long line of artists and designers, so it goes without saying that art—and more importantly, the need to create art—is in my blood.

My Earliest Influences

My grandmother Helen Brown was a gifted seamstress who was known for her delicate handmade lace and beautiful quilts. In her hometown of Bandera, Texas, she was also famous for her hand-tailored Western shirts worn during the spectacular cowboy and cowgirl parades of the 1930s and 40s, complete with embroidered snail trails (that's what we called the embroidered designs), monograms, and pearl snap buttons.

My other grandmother, Louise, was a wily old antiques dealer. Her store, Louise's Antiques, was the most eclectic antiques shop in San Antonio, Texas. She had a knack for finding the most amazing things, and many times would sell them right out of the trunk of her car before she had a chance to unload them into her store.

Even though she had a good eye for finding treasures, she wasn't as confident about displaying them. She would have me come in and fix the displays and decorate the store for her in exchange for candy money. The two of us

An antique bronze angel stands guard over the dining room.

worked as a team from about the time I was ten until I was eighteen. I would also accompany my grandmother on buying trips, and she taught me how to sift through the junk at estate sales to find the real treasures.

Because Louise was pretty well known in the antiques world for spotting priceless heirlooms, it became progressively harder for her to move around at shows and estate sales without being recognized. Sometimes people would grab what she was looking at and buy it first, or dealers would name a higher price than they'd originally planned when selling to her. As a result, she began sending me ahead of her to scout out the good loot before anyone else knew what was going on. If I offered up some cheap piece of junk, I could tell pretty quickly from the look on her face that it was worthless. So from an early age, I learned to distinguish between treasures and trash, a skill that is crucial to the success of Magnolia Pearl.

Another person who influenced my style was my great-aunt Helen. She was an interior decorator who told me, "A room isn't complete without something Oriental in it." Objects from the Far East work well with the Magnolia Pearl style because, like the Victorian style I love, they possess richness, opulence, and attention to detail. I am particularly drawn to

OPPOSITE: A Victorian magazine stand, French tufted-velvet mohair chair, Italian wall sconces, and a Magnolia Pearl travel bag (lower right) create an opulent tableau.

Asian furniture, embroidered silks, carved jewelry, and of course, China dishes and tea sets. Handmade objects from days gone by just speak to my soul. They tell a poignant story about a time when beautiful things were valued above time and money.

My Parents

For whatever skills and talents I have, whether learned or inherited, the two people I consider the most influential were my parents, Anna Thurmond and Preston Brown. They were true artists in every sense of the word. Anna Thurmond was a beautiful gypsy with strong Native American features. In addition to being a go-go dancer at a bar in Hollywood, where she would hang out after work having drinks with the likes of Janis Joplin, Anna was also a brilliant textile artist, which is why I have always been drawn to working with fabrics and textures. In fact, I was designing dresses and purses at an age when other kids were blowing spit bubbles and playing hopscotch.

During my childhood, my mother would often take me to the *ropa usadas* on the Mexican border. At these "rag factories," vintage fabrics and old clothes were sold by the pound. We would spend the day digging through piles of damp, smelly fabric in the sauna-like warehouses, and then return home with loads of vintage clothing and materials for my mother to use in her sewing projects. She would

OPPOSITE LEFT: Robin at age five in a polka-dotted dress of her own design (really!) with her father, Preston Brown, and the Easter Bunny.

OPPOSITE CENTER: Robin's great-aunt Helen Norris.

OPPOSITE RIGHT: Robin's mother, Anna Thurmond, creating art in her natural environment.

take a shirt or a coat completely apart and redesign it, sometimes adding lace or changing the buttons. Then she would sew it back together, never once using a tape measure to accomplish her task. Somehow, everything always came out even and symmetrical. Needless to say, my mom made most of my clothes, and that played a large part in where I got my sense of style. Anna was also a purse maker, and she liked to make mosaic pictures and religious themed scenes out of all kinds of materials to decorate the purses while my father would make handles for them out of driftwood.

My father, Preston Brown, walked that fine line between madman and genius. Both of my parents were driven to create art, but Preston could hardly speak a single sentence without talking about art. He was primarily a painter, but practically every act he committed was an art project of some sort. He didn't make a lot of demands on me other than encouraging me to be passionate and create something beautiful every day. He used to tell me that if you weren't creating something beautiful, then you weren't worthy of being here. "The only thing you need to create art is an imagination," he would say.

Victorian Splendor and Peacocks

When I was six, my brother, Thovas, was born, and we moved from Hollywood to Sebastopol, California. Two years later, we moved to nearby Forestville. My parents got a job as caretakers of a five-hundred-acre ranch with an old Victorian house on it where we lived. The house was so old it didn't have a bathroom in it, but it was a beautiful, two-story home with a wraparound porch downstairs, another porch upstairs, and old wood floors that creaked when you walked. It had belonged to someone's great-aunt, and she had left everything there, so the place was lavishly furnished with Victorian antiques, colorful tapestries, Oriental rugs, velvet curtains, crystal chandeliers, and a grand piano. There were decades of accumulated stuff in that home, and that's where my love affair with the Victorian style truly began. All the different textures were alluring. I felt comfortable in that kind of décor. Since then, I have always tried to recreate that feeling of warmth through the combination of textures.

There was also one other thing on this ranch: peacocks . . . about four hundred of them, to be exact. To me, this was just about the closest thing to heaven on earth. Imagine beautiful rolling hills of yellow daffodils and the iridescent purples, blues, and greens of hundreds of peacocks swarming down those hills. You can understand the effect that would have on somebody's color sense later on in life.

But wait, the story gets better.

I loved playing with the peacocks, and my father officially made me their caretaker. I figured out that peacocks loved cat food, and I could get them to follow me around wherever I went. I would walk around in my oversized silk kimono with the pockets stuffed to the brim with kibble, herding them closer and closer to the house with a stick, until one day they were in the house. To me, this was the most beautiful sight: peacocks on all the furniture, brightly colored tails hanging down the stove, birds walking up and down the stairs, all the while calling out to each other in that haunting, lonely way. I couldn't wait for my father to get home so that I could show him my accomplishment.

According to my dad, it just so happened that he came home that day feeling a little . . . "psychedelic." When he walked into the house and saw me standing in the middle of an ocean of peacocks, wearing my billowy robe and holding a stick in my hand with my mother's rings on every finger, he said I looked like I was a thou-

Robin with her friend, Pandora Keyes, and her brother, Thovas Brown.

OPPOSITE: One of the many peacocks that grace Robin and John's home.

sand years old—like some ancient, gnarled peacock herder with gray hair. He hastily told me to evict my flock of feathered friends and got to work cleaning the "fowl" mess made on my mother's prized chamber stove. On that day, my father and I came to an agreement that a peacock's place is in the yard!

Of course, for an imaginative young girl like me, all those lovely peacock feathers were an obvious invitation to make art . . . or a profit. I suppose I should mention at this point that at the time, I really loved candy. I was a sugar junkie, and I would do anything to get my fix. But candy costs money and I hatched an ingenious scheme to get it. I came up with the idea to make "peacock pencils" that I could sell to my friends at school. In order to get the necessary feathers, I would quietly sneak up behind an unsuspecting bird and pluck out a tail feather with a quick jerk. I would then shave the wood from a real pencil and slowly insert the lead into the quill. Just like that, I had a bona fide peacock pencil!

I sold my peacock pencils to every kid in my class for ten cents apiece. You would look out over the class and there was a kaleidoscopic sea of colorful feathers dancing and swaying in the air as the kids were writing. When my father found out that I was pulling the feathers from the birds' tails, he wasn't happy. But I was too blazed on sugar from the candy cigarettes, wax lips, saltwater taffy, and candy necklaces to care. However, I did learn a valuable lesson from my peacock pencil enterprise: Imagination and creativity can lead to not only personal fulfillment, but entrepreneurial success, as well.

The Government Cheese Years

As the 1970s rolled around, my family moved to San Antonio, Texas, to be closer to my grandparents. These were the "Government Cheese Years," as my brother and I would later call them. You see, art wasn't a particularly hot commodity in Texas during the 1970s, so my parents, who were not really interested in climbing the social ladder, were almost literally starving artists. We were so poor we had to use food stamps, so in effect, the government fed us. The cheese stood out because it was really oily and behaved in a most uncheeselike manner. It tasted so horrible, and it wouldn't even melt—no gooey, grilled cheese sandwiches for Thovas and me. We were grateful at least to have food, but as a young child, it's sometimes hard to understand why you have to eat what you do.

Not long after arriving in Texas, my parents opened the first rock-and-roll vintage merchandise store in San Antonio, called "Banana Funk and Junk." Every square inch of the store was covered with my dad's paintings and art, including the murals he painted on the walls. My mother constructed one-of-a-kind wearable creations using vintage fabrics. In addition, they sold funky chandeliers, lampshades, furniture that my mom re-upholstered, tattered lace, and worn Oriental rugs. Most of the things in the store were objects they had found and fixed up. Unfortunately, it was all a little bit too funky for the conservative Texans of the time, so "Banana Funk and Junk" closed after only a few years.

During the Banana Funk and Junk years, we worked together as a family hunting for hidden treasures at the rag factories, flea markets, yard sales, and even the city dump. With nothing more than our imagination and some elbow grease, we were able to create wearable works of art and unique furnishings. Through this experience, I learned that one of my greatest contributions in this life would be creative inspiration.

Since my family was so poor, we had a tendency to move around a lot. No matter what cockroach-infested place we moved into, the first thing Anna and Preston did was transform the place into something akin to the Taj Mahal (if the Taj Mahal had been decorated by Timothy Leary). My brother and I scavenged the alleys and vacant lots, looking for discarded junk to take back to our parents to help fix up the place. My mother sewed curtains and recovered furniture that other people had discarded, while my father would set all kinds of funky shapes in the walls with a saw and paint murals on the walls, ceilings, and floors. The place would become beautiful practically overnight.

Every day was a lesson in being creative and resourceful. Just because we didn't have any money to go out and buy all kinds of expensive things didn't mean we couldn't have nice things. My parents just relied on their artistic creativity to make our homes beautiful. And they showed me that any dwelling could be made into a beautiful home if you exercise a little creativity. When you combine my parents' inventive brilliance and the way they raised us with my own artistic inclinations, you get Magnolia Pearl.

"Every day was a lesson in being creative and resourceful. Just because we didn't have any money to go out and buy all kinds of expensive things didn't mean we couldn't have nice things.**"**

Even as a child, Robin was captivated by the many different shades of colors found in nature. Today, she constantly returns to nature for color inspiration.

My Life in Layers

> ART IS ABOUT THE PROCESS, NOT THE PRODUCT. DON'T BE ATTACHED TO THE OUTCOME. REFLECT GOD AND FEED THE SOUL. THAT IS THE TRUEST MEANING OF ART.

In addition to the Victorian fringe, this couch features French curtain panels, Belgian lace, European cut velvet, Polish embroidered tapestries, and damask.

OPPOSITE: The guest house bedroom houses layer upon layer of textured fabrics. Robin is not inhibited when it comes to combining colors and patterns and you shouldn't be either.

ON SOME LEVEL, I THINK I'VE ALWAYS BEEN A DESIGNER. Even as a child of ten, I made my own unusual outfits complete with cute little purses made from scraps of old fabric, denim and lace. (Obviously, in my family, we couldn't afford to buy department store clothes—and with our hippie sensibility, we wouldn't have wanted to wear them anyway!) As a teenager, I continued to design my own clothes and develop my own funky retro style. While everyone else was strutting around in preppy clothes with designer labels, I was wearing floor-length gowns made out of old overalls, and jeans adorned with velvet bell-bottoms, embroidery, and lace. In my outlandish apparel, I definitely stood out from the crowd, and while most of the kids didn't know what to make of me, others thought my look was pretty cool and asked me to embellish their clothing, too.

During the early 1980s, my interest in Victorian furnishings continued to develop as I helped my grandmother in her San Antonio antique shop. I set up furniture on the floor and designed elaborate window displays. Grandmother Louise was a truly remarkable lady and I really cherish my memories of working with her. Through that experience, I learned so much about the antique business and decorating techniques—lessons I still use to this day.

One of the most important milestones of that time took place in 1987 when I met the love of my life, John Gray. It was at an outdoor reggae musical event in downtown San Antonio. I like to tell people it was "love at first dance," and we've been best friends and soulmates ever since!

In my mid-twenties, I discovered that I could actually make a living from my talents when a private school in San Antonio hired me to teach art. I found that I absolutely loved working with children! Later, I worked with the elderly at an assisted living residence that John operated in South Texas. I led some really special classes in watercolor painting, embroidery, and quilt making. I can honestly say that while working with children and older folks, they taught me just as much as I taught them about the creative process and the simple joy of art.

Magnolia Pearl is the name of the interior design and fashion business that John and I started from our home in the beautiful Texas Hill Country town of Bandera. John and I share a love of old, beautiful things. Together we comb flea markets, thrift stores, antique stores, and estate sales in search of treasures to decorate our home: old paintings by unknown artists, ravaged Victorian furniture, alabaster lamps and broken chandeliers, cracked vases,

John Gray and Robin Brown.

vintage jewelry, salvaged rugs and tapestries, mismatched dishes and tarnished silverware. It doesn't necessarily matter how dilapidated or worn something is; the beauty of many objects transcends their surface condition—sometimes they're even beautiful because of it. And besides, just because something is broken, doesn't mean it has to be fixed. Our home just seems to make sense the way it's decorated— everything blends together seamlessly. Every time you come to our home there is some new-old object to behold.

OPPOSITE: This fantastic bird house was created by Robin and John and is covered with hundreds of seashells.

My Move to the Hill Country

Magnolia Pearl started to materialize in the late 1990s, when it became clear that we were in need of bigger digs. Our comfortable little house on Pecan Street was quickly outgrowing our cornucopia of ramshackle treasures. Fortunately, we came upon an old farmhouse for sale that was in desperate need of attention and seemed to fit our needs perfectly. It was spacious and open, sat on 40 acres, and there were a couple of outbuildings that could be used as guest cottages. Fixing up the house was not going to be easy, but at least we had the opportunity to add, renovate, and rebuild it according to our wants and needs.

Our home was actually the original cafeteria building for the old school in Bandera. I was told that it was transported out to the country by covered wagon by the family that first lived here. Decades later, another owner modernized the place with nice, new windows, doors, and roof, and then we came along and ripped everything out and started from scratch! We wanted to restore the house to its original condition, so we used salvaged materials for our doors, windows, and wall coverings, both inside and out. During the process of renovation, our priority was maintaining the architectural style and design elements of the period. The result is that a visit to our home feels like a step back in time. It's a truly magical place that's perfect for the life John and I have created. I can sincerely say that I hope to grow old in our little Hill Country home.

OPPOSITE: A move to the Hill Country allowed Magnolia Pearl to grow and flourish. The exterior of the house is covered with old ceiling tin and metal architectural pieces that bring the art of layering outside. The table and chair are faux bois, a traditional French art form that uses concrete to simulate old wood.

Robin's garden is filled with the wildflowers for which the Texas Hill Country is so famous.

Although we had no intention of starting an interior decorating business when we began working on the house, it turned out to be the beginnings of Magnolia Pearl. At the time, we were just making a place to live for ourselves. And because we rebuilt the entire house, the interior spaces were blank canvases begging to be painted. The concept of layering, while not yet formally named or recognized, was the only way of decorating that made any kind of sense to me. Layering seemed like the most natural and normal way to display all the beautiful things that we had accumulated (and, believe me, there were a lot).

Around this time, in 2001, my mother passed away. My father had passed away in 1997, and so now I felt an overwhelming responsibility to continue their artistic lineage, and to make sure the family creativity didn't die along with them. I had always been creative and artistic, but I didn't allow it to come into full bloom while my parents were alive. Even though they encouraged me to engage myself in any and all artistic endeavors, I believed that they were the true artistic stars and I didn't feel comfortable in a situation if it might mean that I would outshine them.

Inspiration Dawns

I had an old tapestry of Jesus that my mother had gotten from France, and the night she died, I had an epiphany to fashion a purse from it to honor my mother. A few days later when John and I were at the grocery store, a woman saw me with my purse. She followed us around and kept asking about the purse—was it for sale? I politely said no, and told her why I'd made the purse, explaining its sentimental value. The woman understood, but was very persistent and offered me a substantial sum of money on the spot. I talked it over with John for a bit and decided that since I needed money to pay for my mom's funeral, I couldn't say no, even though it pained me greatly. It occurred to me that taking the skills and talents I inherited from my parents and turning them into an opportunity to commit one final act for my mother would be a fitting way to honor her life and celebrate taking up the family's artistic torch. I sold the purse.

Going into Business

Filled with cathartic inspiration, I went home and made another purse. This time several different women approached me, intent on buying it right off my back. It was John who realized that I might have hit upon something with my "little crafts," as he jokingly called them. We raced home to get to work producing more purses.

Robin finds beauty in the smallest things, like flower blossoms, velvet ribbons, and vintage jewelry.

OPPOSITE: Take notice of all the beautiful colors in Mother Nature's palette, then let it inspire your design choices. Robin created this sunny backpack for hauling booty around at the antique shows.

A good friend of ours, Todd Hallmark, happened to be visiting for a couple of weeks while all this was going on, and he realized that this could be a really successful business if we were willing to take it to the next level. That next level, however, required a considerable amount of money—something Todd was willing to provide. I immediately bought a load of vintage textiles, brooches, and trim with my newly acquired capital. I worked endlessly cutting and designing purses, perfecting my style. Just like before, every time I was out in public with one of my purses, people would follow me and almost demand that I sell it to them. Then, as they walked around with their new Magnolia Pearl creation, they'd get inundated with requests to know where the bag came from and would direct more people my way. There were numerous occasions when swarms of people clamored to buy a purse right out of the trunk of our car. I would never have believed my "little crafts" could cause such a stir.

So in the beginning, my business really was built by "word of mouth." However, it didn't take long for the press to get wind of what I was doing. Soon feature articles and photo spreads were being published in national magazines such as *Country Living*. I also made some guest appearances on local television shows in San Antonio. Thanks to all the publicity, my phone was ringing off the wall with orders for my handmade bags. At the time, customers had to rely on my descriptions of the bags to make their purchases, but after I launched my website in 2002, folks could see the available inventory for themselves and order on-line. Today, my bags are sold in a few upscale boutiques and exclusive antique

Shelves piled high with vintage fabrics and textiles Robin has collected over time.

shows such as Marburger Farms in Round Top, Texas. And of course, anyone willing to make the trek to the boondocks of Bandera County is always welcome. Our studio is in a century-old cotton gin that John and I bought in nearby Medina, Texas, and re-assembled right on the ranch.

People often ask me how I came up with the name Magnolia Pearl. Well, here's the inside story on how it all

OPPOSITE: She sells sea shells by the front door.

came together: The magnolia has always been one of our family emblems. My great-grandfather Robert Brown was a civil engineer who oversaw construction of the Magnolia Petroleum Building in Dallas, Texas. And then, believe it or not, I was actually born on Magnolia Street in San Antonio. As a teenager, the first painting I ever sold was of—you guessed it—a magnolia. The magnolia thing just keeps popping up in my life. And then I've always had an affinity for pearls. Even as a child, I draped myself in strands and strands of pearls, and "Pearl" naturally became my nickname. So you see, the name "Magnolia Pearl" is the perfect match for me, the company, and my creative vision.

Magnolia Pearl Expands

The success of the purses allowed me to add a clothing line to the Magnolia Pearl label. I had always designed clothes for myself, and now I had the opportunity to dress the women that had been such ardent fans of my purses. I bought new and vintage fabrics from Italy, France, and Belgium to create my bohemian-Victorian style of women's clothing. I started creating beautiful bloomers, blouses, bed jackets, and lace dresses out of hand-dyed velvets, silks, brocades, and lace. John and I spent hours (as we still do today) drawing designs on each individual article of clothing that was to be lavishly hand-embroidered. Magnolia Pearl Couture is what Victorian style would have been if Queen Victoria had partied with Janis Joplin and Alice in Wonderland.

As more and more people started to come over to our house to try on clothes and buy purses, they would see the furniture that I had designed and want to buy the pieces for themselves. As you will see from the photographs, and the details in Chapter Eight, my furniture is just as over-the-top as the other Magnolia Pearl designs. In fact, all the materials I buy are used in every facet of Magnolia Pearl.

LEFT: Robin's grandfather, Preston Brown, and grandmother, Helen Brown.

OPPOSITE: The perfect combination of inspiration and design—a Magnolia Pearl bag is filled with flowers.

OPPOSITE: Robin's back porch features a mosaic carpet wall paired elegantly with Magnolia Pearl couture furniture and a vase with flowers.

LEFT: Robin applied four different pieces of carpet and strips of tin to this section of the wall and topped it off with two old pairs of deer antlers. The painting, with its weathered frame, is a flea market treasure.

Layering

When pressed to come up with a notion of how I decorate a room, I think I finally hit upon what it is that defines my style. It's that no one thing stands out among the others. Each object and facet of decorating could stand alone on its own merit. But when placed together, they function as a cohesive unit. It dawned on me that my style features layer upon layer of beauty. You can look past one object to another, and then look past that object to another, and so on, until it just sort of hits you that you are completely surrounded by art and beauty. This layered effect is responsible for the lush and lavish look of Magnolia Pearl.

How else can I describe layering? It's almost like decorating your decorations—or as we say in Texas, putting a hat on top of a hat. One of the tenets of my art is "don't be afraid to cover beauty with more beauty." The result will be a depth and coziness that you don't find too often in homes. A lot of times you hear the modernist mantra "less is more." Other times, you hear decorators say, "more is more." I say "more is never enough." Never. But when I say "never," I mean never consider yourself finished with the layering process. Keep on looking for beautiful things and changing things around. But don't just keep adding endlessly to what you've already got, because then what you'll have is clutter. You don't walk around our home tripping over everything; the art of layering is a lot of things, but cluttered is definitely not one of them.

OPPOSITE: The salvage mentality is about recycling treasures that have soul and beauty. Here, old wood columns and lace panels create the illusion of division within a small space.

An alabaster bust of Diana, the goddess of hunting, protects some of Robin's favorite treasures: Pearls from her grandmother Louise, a cameo from her great-aunt Helen, and a seashell given to her by her father when she was a child. All of the treasures sit on top of a marble-topped music cabinet.

An embellishment could go on a purse . . . or end up on a sofa; a vintage tapestry could be used on a chair . . . or end up on a jacket.

With the throng of women visiting our farmhouse to buy clothes, purses, and now furniture, there also came a demand for me to decorate their homes. People from all around who seemed to appreciate my style were asking me to help them get the Magnolia Pearl look for their homes.

Choose Beauty

A conglomeration of junk isn't going to manifest into the Magnolia Pearl style. You need to know when to acquire something when to resist, and also when to give it away. Each individual piece you display should be able to stand alone as an object of beauty. One beautiful piece is better than fifty bland ones.

How do I define beauty? I like to use a famous line by John Keats: "Beauty is truth; truth beauty." Beauty is undeniable. Of course, it is relative, too. It's different things for different people. You have to develop your own eye for beauty, and that is something I can't stress enough. If something stops you in your tracks and takes your breath away, that's a good sign that you find it beautiful.

The one common thread shared by nearly all things that I consider beautiful is that they are handmade. There is very little that was mass-produced in our home. Magnolia Pearl is about celebrating art and artist and surrounding yourself with beautiful handmade things that tell a story. Mass-produced objects too often feel lifeless and without soul. The salvage mentality is about recycling treasures that have soul and beauty. Try surrounding yourself with things that were painstakingly created with someone's heart, hands, and soul.

> **"**Think about a lump of clay that a child brings home that is supposed to be a vase or an ashtray (or both). It's treasured because it expresses someone's love. It's proudly displayed and brings a smile to your heart. That's what I am talking about.**"**

Think about the object in your home that you love. This plaster goddess adorned with pearls appeals to Robin's sense of beauty.

Now, the concept of what I am preaching is to seek out originality—in your own style. It just happens that mine is bohemian-Victoriental funk because of the things that have influenced me. That may not be for you. When you buy things to decorate your home, you are essentially saying, "These things are who I am and what I am all about." What about being different and unique?

Think about the objects in your home that you love. Did they come from one of those big national stores that sell mass-produced things? The answer is probably no.

Rules? What rules? Who made the rules anyway? Make your own.

Everything in my home feels like it belongs there. All the rules of conventional design and decorating have been swept out my door like yesterday's dust. However, that doesn't mean that there aren't rules to the Magnolia Pearl style. Well, maybe not rules . . . more like fundamental elements.

* Don't be afraid to cover beauty with beauty. This is what defines the art of layering.

* The art of layering is the art of noncompletion; it's never really finished. Part of the fun is constantly rotating and changing out items and rearranging furniture. Have fun with it seasonally . . . or heck, daily.

* Don't get bogged down by convention. Don't be intimidated by what other people think about your style or let their negative opinions keep you from decorating your own home the way you want to, even if it may be outrageous. It's your home; express yourself.

* You can never have too many beautiful things. You might not want your house to be stuffed so full that you can't walk through it. But you can build lots of layers with lots of little details, ensuring each piece has its own intrinsic value and beauty. Collections are okay, but don't own nine hundred ceramic frog figurines—unless you really dig frogs.

* Think *hecho a mano* (no, that doesn't mean "to heck with the man," it means "made by hand"). Allow more handmade things into your home and weed out the mass-produced things. Create art for art's sake. It's like a child drawing a picture: They do it just for the love of drawing. Celebrate art and artist.

* Incorporate as many textures, colors, materials, and patterns as you like, but the look should be cohesive and it should all work together without obvious effort.

RIGHT: Multiple light sources create ambiance: An alabaster Grecian globe hangs overhead while a Victorian floor lamp lights a corner behind the sofa. Note the soft natural light coming from the window on the left and one off camera to the right.

OPPOSITE: Three bronze maidens stand guard over other Victorian treasures on top of a carpet-covered cabinet.

The things we tend to love are things we find when we go on vacation or that are family heirlooms, and you probably have a great story to tell about them. There is a sense of pride because these things are unique to you.

By applying the salvage mentality to your everyday life, you can feed your soul. Start going to antique stores and thrift stores more often. Driving by a garage sale or yard sale? Stop your car and check it out. You might find something that you absolutely love. Look in the newspaper for estate sales and auctions, and don't be intimidated by them. You can find great bargains there. You'll learn more about this in the next chapter, which is devoted to the art of salvaging.

One of the things that can happen when you feed your soul is that you start to trust your own instincts more. You'll start thinking more about what you truly love—what really defines you—not just things, but thoughts and deeds as well. You won't be just another lemming doing a cannonball off the cliff into a sea of mediocrity. You will start to develop your own decorating skills, and who knows? Maybe you will discover your inner creative genius.

In most decorating styles, you are told that there are rules for grouping objects, rules for placing objects, rules on the use of colors, and rules for blah blah blah. Not here, not now. As you hone and begin to trust your decorating skills, I hope that you will define your own rules along the way, as they apply to your home.

The art of layering is not an overnight project. Be patient. You're looking for quality, and that's increasingly rare these days. Take your time—you will be rewarded for it. I believe our home is the perfect example of what I mean by "the art of layering." You see, it was a blank canvas when we bought it in 1997, so we started with a good foundation of salvaged wood and etched tin for the walls and ceilings. Then we had a friend, Christina Blackledge, paint the interior walls with murals of flowers, birds, and other natural elements. We surrounded her artwork with layers of fabrics in varying shades and textures. For window treatments, we used old, crocheted lace. The hardwood floors were layered with colorful rugs of all styles. When we began furnishing the home, we had the opportunity to add even more layers of fabric. Of course, our Victorian furniture is upholstered in cut velvets, needlepoint, and brocade. And to top it all off we have tons of big, comfy pillows adorned with tassels and metallic trim. The effect is a lush, opulent atmosphere that conveys comfort and luxury at the same time. Be advised though that layering is always a work in progress and a little addictive. For instance, in our home, I'm afraid that we may have just reached the saturation point for layering. But then again, I can always switch materials and experiment with new decorating combinations. That's the fun of layering!

Life is an acquired taste. As you start to acquire new tastes for new things, the layering begins.

OPPOSITE: This Magnolia Pearl Couture couch is covered with vintage damask, French curtain panels, Belgian lace, European cut velvet, and embroidered tapestries from Poland. Robin's philosophy? Don't be afraid to cover beauty with more beauty.

Trash to Treasure

"INSPIRATION FROM OTHERS IS FINE, BUT THE BEST INSPIRATION COMES FROM YOUR OWN IMAGINATION . . . WE ALL HAVE ONE!"

MY FATHER HAD A PEACOCK-BLUE TRIUMPH motorcycle that he used to love riding all over Hollywood, often times accompanied by a certain little blond-haired girl wearing a hot pink paisley dress and white go-go boots. Because I was so small, I had to ride between his arms, straddling the gas tank. Together, we would cruise around town, riding to the park for a picnic or to the beach for a walk in the water. Strolling along the beach was one of my favorite pastimes because I loved to find things in the sand to use as materials for art projects, such as driftwood and old sea-glass. The

LEFT: A walk through Robin's garden finds many vintage treasures put to unexpected use, like an old manual typewriter that now serves as a planter.

OPPOSITE: Robin traded her friend Don Yarton a set of crewelwork curtain panels for this gorgeous brass ceiling medallion. The French crystal chandelier that hangs from it reminds Robin of something that would have been found on the *Titanic*.

shards of broken bottles were worn smooth from years of tumbling in the ocean, so to me, they were like beautiful little blue and green jewels. I used my beachcombing discoveries to decorate picture frames, jewelry, and keepsake boxes—things I could put in my room as daily reminders of special time with my dad.

When I talk about salvaging, I'm talking about rescuing things from going to waste and then giving them a new purpose in life. Of course, you shouldn't hold on to every little scrap you come across. Some objects won't be

For vintage light fixtures in which the bulbs are visible, choose reproduction Edison-style bulbs or candelabra bulbs like these.

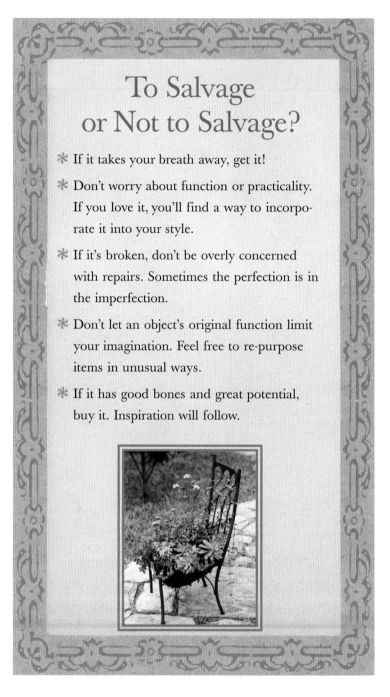

To Salvage or Not to Salvage?

✳ If it takes your breath away, get it!

✳ Don't worry about function or practicality. If you love it, you'll find a way to incorporate it into your style.

✳ If it's broken, don't be overly concerned with repairs. Sometimes the perfection is in the imperfection.

✳ Don't let an object's original function limit your imagination. Feel free to re-purpose items in unusual ways.

✳ If it has good bones and great potential, buy it. Inspiration will follow.

to your taste, and others should be left for the trashman. Ignoring things you don't like and the trash is usually pretty easy. Those things usually don't have anything to say to you. But how do you discern whether something potentially promising, something hidden under dirt and grime, say, is salvageworthy? Good question.

If an object catches your eye or your heart kind of skips a beat, you need to take a closer look. Take time to investigate it in detail. If it speaks to you—if it looks like it has a story to tell—it just might be worth salvaging. Again, let your instinct be your guide. If it makes you feel good, then you will probably enjoy having it in your home. Don't be too concerned with chips, dings, scratches, or peeling paint. A bit of rust is usually not a big deal. Little imperfections can enhance the story, and a lot of times are a big part of what makes an object beautiful. Sometimes, you can clean or refinish a piece and make it nearly as good as new. Missing parts can often be rebuilt or replaced, and electrical items with frayed cords can be rewired. Don't let a little hard work keep you from something you love. One of the great things about salvaging discarded items is that they often cost you next to nothing, other than a little time.

Be on the lookout for discarded items; you'll be surprised at what people get rid of. If you don't have that salvage mentality, it may take a while to hone it. There's no telling what you may have passed up if you're not used to salvaging. Some of the most beautiful pieces of furniture in my home started out as a find on the street. I've brought home dilapidated pieces of furniture that looked like they had already given up the best that they had to offer, and with a little bit of work, they now look as though

the best is here and now. I've taken old dressers that had good bones but bad skin, and performed minor reconstructive surgery with a ratty Oriental rug, a few nails, and some new drawer pulls. I found a trashed-out Victorian loveseat for a friend that had broken legs, a loose back, and shredded upholstery with springs poking out, and I made it look brand new by covering it with shimmering deep blue tufted velvet and giving it new legs.

I have rescued so many things from the trash heap and given them new life that I have proven that you *can* get something for nothing; all it takes is a little imagination and ingenuity. If you find yourself running a little short on imagination, however, or don't feel comfortable picking up

The circular back panel of this ornate Victorian settee is covered with beautifully embroidered Chinese silk, velvet and lace ribbons, and French silk flowers.

other people's trash, there are plenty of other salvaging opportunities. We all have that hunter-gatherer instinct; you just need to know where to seek your prey.

Tiptoe through the tulips to yard sales, antique shows, auctions, and estate sales; search online; go to thrift stores and antique stores. It's exciting to search out places and opportunities where you can find unusual, one-of-kind treasures for your home. This is the thrill of the hunt.

Antique Shows

Antique shows are an absolute must for anyone wanting to develop the Magnolia Pearl style, and they are a blast! Check your local newspaper or online to locate antique shows in your area—there's a list of shows across the country on page 150.

The Marburger Farm Antique Show is held semiannually during round Top Antiques Week in Southeast Texas.

For outdoor events, you'll want to bring a lunch, some water, sunscreen, comfortable shoes, and a few of your close friends, and go! Our favorite is the Warrenton-Round Top Show in Texas. It's a two-week long festival with shows in the spring and fall. It's open to the public, and vendors from all around the world set up booths inside huge circus tents. It's elegantly and beautifully done, and you wouldn't believe the things you can find there. I was visiting the tent that had antiques from France and saw a twenty-five-foot-tall statue of the Venus de Milo—it sold for thirty thousand dollars in about five minutes. Of course there are plenty of more affordable (and portable) deals to be found there, so don't be intimidated. The nicest and most exclusive show to get into at Warrenton is John Sauls's Marburger Farm Antique Show. It lasts for five days and also happens to include Magnolia Pearl's fashion and furniture.

At the Marburger Farm Antique Show this antique chandelier attracted the attention of *Country Living* Editor in Chief Nancy Soriano and editors Nicole Esposito Polly and Frances Bailey.

LEFT: According to show founder John Sauls, hard-core buyers come to Marburger early. But so many vendors bring such an abundance of goods, late-in-the-day shoppers will still find a wealth of great stuff.

ABOVE: Robin shows her custom couture furniture, like this opulent chair, as well as her fashion at her Marburger booth.

OPPOSITE: The back porch of Robin and John's home is often a gathering place for their peacocks.

Auctions and Estate Sales

These are huge, one-time possibilities to find some real treasures, and it can take a bit of work. In most areas, there is a group of area auctioneers or auction houses. You can put yourself on their mailing lists to be notified about upcoming auctions and estate sales. You can also check your local newspapers for information. Many auctions and estate sales have previews so you can go ahead of time to see what is being sold and if you want anything. Also, most of these events are cash and carry—you have to take the object with you when you leave—so by going to the preview, you'll know if you should arrange for special transportation to haul back your loot. Timing is everything, so get there early. Auctions can be an exciting way to spend the day, even if you don't buy. Also keep in mind that sometimes the crowd gets tired as the auction goes on, so stay for the duration; you can often get good deals at the end.

Thrift Stores and Antique Stores

Both are good places to find cool things for decorating your home, with thrift stores selling more low-end collectible things and antiques stores selling, well, antiques. Depending on what you are looking for, both places can be good resources for salvaging. The most important thing to remember about both is that they're constantly getting new stuff in. You can't just go once and think you've seen all they have to offer. Also, by going often, you develop a rapport with the owners, who might call you to let you know if they spot something you would like.

OPPOSITE: Let them eat lace!

There is one other aspect of salvaging that is important to consider: the art of trading. I have an insatiable appetite for beautiful things. In fact, I'll readily admit I'm addicted to them. When I fall in love with something, I have to have it (within reason, of course). But as I said before, the Magnolia Pearl style is not about clutter, and I can't keep bringing new things into my home without getting rid of other things at the same time. This is where trading comes in.

Silverware too worn and bent to eat with makes a rustic wind chime in Robin's yard.

The Art of Trading

Through my collecting journeys, I've kind of had a tendency to "upgrade" the things I have. Most antique dealers are buy-sell-trade . . . the key word in this case being trade. If they have something you really want, and you have something they want, then you might be able to work out a deal that's beneficial to both of you. Maybe sometime you'll want to trade several of your things for one really nice thing that's a little more expensive. Then later on down the line, you might take that nice thing in, along with a bunch of other stuff, and trade again. See? Upgrading. It's another good reason to start developing relationships with antique dealers and shop owners.

One of my favorite trades involves a deal I made with antique dealer and good friend, Don Yarton. He was in the market for some old crewel-work curtain panels and I had been searching for the perfect ceiling medallion to mount above the chandelier in our living room. He presented me with a beautiful, six-foot-wide, brass medallion that was made in France—and I swapped the curtains

for it before he could change his mind! Seriously, a good trade isn't about "getting the best" of the other guy or getting something for nothing. It's about knowing that the objects will be used, enjoyed, and appreciated more by their new owner. You know, they say a perfect compromise is when both sides are dissatisfied, but I believe the perfect trade happens when both parties go home happy.

No matter what, it's important to always try to acquire good quality things. The more you learn and know about antiques, the better off you are. You can't bargain with someone if you don't know what you are bargaining for. Figure out what you like and then study it; find out what it sells for in certain conditions. Learn the names of things so you know what to ask for. Ask questions! Then search online or at a bookstore for more answers. Salvaging can be very rewarding, and you will become passionate about it. Like everything else in life, it is best shared with friends who have the same passion—unless, of course, they are looking for the same antiques you are.

OPPOSITE: No part of Robin's house is overlooked for decoration. Here on the front porch, lace overhangs an antique cast-iron fireplace door illuminated by an old chandelier.

A Good Fountation: The First Layer

A SMART WOMAN IS NOT A WOMAN WHO CAN DO EVERYTHING; A SMART WOMAN IS A WOMAN CAN GET EVERYTHING DONE. SHARE THE PROJECT.

ONE DAY WHEN I WAS ABOUT TWELVE, my father and I were walking down by the river near McAllister Freeway in San Antonio. He was telling me that I was surrounded by art; all I had to do was give birth to it. To make his point, he scooped up a handful of red claylike rocks from the banks of the river and proceeded to draw a mural on the side of the freeway embankment. It took him all day, but when he was done, the entire concrete structure was covered with this beautiful red clay drawing of the San Antonio River surrounded by a sunburst, clouds, and twinkling stars. It caused such a stir that the local news stations came down and covered it. You can imagine the impression it made on me at the time, watching my father toil all day in the hot sun making art that would wash off with the first rain.

LEFT: Young Robin with her father.

OPPOSITE: A pair of French vases.

Up until now, I've been talking about the objects that decorate your home, or to use proper decorating terminology, "the stuff." Now it's time to get down to the nitty-gritty of the art of layering. You can go out and buy beautiful treasures to fill your home, display them artfully and thoughtfully, and still not have that layered look unique to Magnolia Pearl. What is the secret, you wonder? I'm glad you asked.

Enhance the foundations of your interior. The walls, windows, ceilings, floor, and doors of a home are as integral the overall design as furnishings, lighting, and accessories. Even the most beautiful antique furniture would look ugly and out of place in a room with bare white walls, fluorescent lighting, and a "popcorn" ceiling. Think of your room as a masterpiece painting. It deserves an equally elaborate frame.

Walls

A Magnolia Pearl wall becomes a decorated canvas before it is adorned with things. The canvas starts by being textured, whether you apply the texture or nature does. I personally prefer to let nature do the work for me, so I use old wood and tin to help start out the layering process with their worn, weathered textures. If all you have is new drywall, that's okay, too; it's all in how you decorate it. Several walls in our home started out as drywall, but you'd never know it now.

No doubt you've all seen decorating books and shows on faux-finishing: Take a rag or a sponge and manipulate the paint to make the walls look like denim or leather or the skin of a South American tree frog, right? Well, we're on the same page—but I don't like the word faux. It

ABOVE AND OPPOSITE: Robin and John removed all the wood siding from the exterior of the house and replaced it with old pressed tin. The weathered exterior wood was used for walls and window trim inside the house.

implies that something is fake, and I don't consider art to be fake. Sure, that wall might not really be covered with denim or leather or frog skin, but the illusion you create can be real art, an expression of your inner self. So look at your wall as a canvas, ready and waiting to be transformed into beautiful art.

One of the most intriguing things about our home is the way the walls themselves stand out as works of art. Some are painted to look like vintage Victorian wallpaper with rows of big magnolia flowers or clusters of roses;

others have peacocks or Chinese Lantern designs. They are all different, and they are all beautiful.

Another wall treatment we love is the application of old carpets to the walls. It's like having the floors on the walls and the result is striking. This makes a good excuse to collect carpets, even if they are beat up and worn. If they *are* worn, good for you! Most people will pass them up, and you can often get them for next to nothing.

In our kitchen, we had a wall that was feeling a little too ordinary. We also had a rug that was beautiful around the borders but kind of blah in the middle, so we decided to fix two problems at the same time. We cut out the blah middle to fit around the doorway in the kitchen. Where two walls met at the corner, we cut the rug and reattached

it to carry it around the other wall. Finally, we cut around one of the more interesting designs in the rug and left the edges exposed to trail off across the wall. You can get the same look in your own home; the important thing to remember is to express your inner artist and have fun with it. It's actually one of the easiest projects in the book, but will probably make the biggest statement in your home.

If cutting up and hanging a carpet seems like too much of a hassle, then why not try layering a wall with lace? Use a water-based glue that dries clear and lace with small holes, then apply the glue to the wall and mosaic the lace in layers until you like the effect. Use the straight edges of the lace around doors and windows, or trim it out with old tin or other pieces of material.

LEFT: Robin's friend Christina Blackledge has painted many of the surfaces of the home, like this mural section.

OPPOSITE: This carpet mosaic wall is the first layer of texture on the porch. Additional elements include tapestry fabrics, a cut-crystal chandelier, and an extraordinary peacock-feather lampshade created by another friend, Binky Morgan.

How to Make a Carpet Mosaic Wall

Inspiration: A lot of old carpets and a big empty wall that needs something different.

How To: Choose carpet that is neither too thick nor really thin. To attach it, you'll need either roofing nails or drywall nails; they typically have a dull finish and a big enough head to hold the carpet. I don't use nails or tacks with big decorative heads because I don't want them to stand out. But if your inner artist tells you to use fancy nails, then listen to that voice.

1. The best wall for this is one covered in wood. If you have that, skip to step 2. If you're working on drywall, you will first need to secure ¼-or ½-inch-thick plywood to the wall, so the weight of the carpet doesn't pull the nails out. Locate the studs behind the drywall either using a little electronic stud-finder (they're not expensive) or by lightly tapping on the wall. It will sound hollow in between the studs, and you'll hear a dull thud when you are on top of a stud. Keep in mind that most studs are spaced 18 to 24 inches apart. Make a small pencil mark on the ceiling where each stud is, then press the plywood against the wall. Using the marks on the ceiling as your guide, screw the plywood into the studs, placing a screw about every 2 feet along the length of the plywood.

2. It's helpful to lay the carpet out flat first. Measure the space you want to cover and find designs to fit that space. A lot of carpets have the most beautiful designs around the corners, edges, and center. Don't be afraid to cut your carpet accordingly, to highlight those designs. Use utility scissors for cutting.

3. Nail the carpet to the wall, starting at the top first. Hammer in a few nails to hold it up, and then fill in with nails every couple of inches. It's important to start at the top, so that gravity can do the majority of the work as you pull the carpet tight and finish nailing. Just go around the border, then up through the body of the carpet. Be sure to keep the carpet tight and smooth as you go along, but don't worry so much about making sure the nails are perfectly symmetrical; it gives it a more artistic, rustic feel if the nail heads are slightly uneven. Where two pieces of carpet come together, you can cut a trim piece from another carpet to hide the seam. Apply more nails than you think you will need, because the carpet will stretch over time and you don't want it to sag.

4. Finally, remember to save your scraps! You never know when they will come in handy for another project.

OPPOSITE: Texture and technique combine for an anything-but-ordinary kitchen, with carpeted walls and cabinet doors hand-painted by Christina Blackledge.

Ceilings

Ceilings are perhaps the most overlooked aspect of decorating, so learning to keep them in mind can do wonders for the look of a room. The first thing I look at is the ceiling. Unlike a floor, which can be covered with rugs, a ceiling requires a little more time and thought. Since I'm going to have a bunch of pretty chandeliers hanging down, people will be looking up, and I don't want the ceiling to clash with the rest of the décor.

Think of the Sistine Chapel with its beautifully painted frescoes. Well, you're probably not going to spend hours on your back painting huge murals on your ceiling—but you could always hire an artist to do it for you if you wanted to.

Another approach would be to cover the ceiling with something textured, like weathered barn wood, bead board, or vintage or reproduction ceiling tin. I'm not talking about the plain-Jane corrugated roofing tin you see on every roadside barbecue shack, I'm talking about beautifully worn, antique pressed ceiling tin. And in this case, old isn't the only way to go. There are a lot of companies making vintage-looking ceiling tin at some pretty amazing prices. If it looks too new, distress it by painting it with a flat-finish paint and antiquing glaze.

Pressed tin is radically valuable to the Magnolia Pearl style because it merges different surfaces together in an

> "No matter what you do, try not to overthink the project—that makes it harder. Remember, it's art; there is no right or wrong. There's only you, and the perfection is in the imperfection. If you don't like the way it looks, pull it down and start over."

artistic way. One of tin's most important features is the depth of relief; the deeper it is, the more striking its effect.

We were fortunate enough to find a bunch of old tin on an online architectural salvage website message board. The man who owned it had just bought a movie theater in New York and was modernizing it, so he had no use for the tin. He also just happened to own his own shipping company, and he shipped it to us for next to nothing. Since we knew the effect that old tin can have on a place, we actually bought the tin before we bought the house. There was so much of it—including the pressed crown molding—the "crème de la trim"—that not only could we cover the entire ceiling inside, but also the complete exterior of the house. It looks phenomenal.

One thing to remember: Whether you paint the ceiling or cover it, don't overlook the air-conditioning vents, if they're up there. Distress them or paint them so they blend in and disappear.

OPPOSITE: The beauty that chandeliers bring to your home cannot be overstated. Even if your decorating budget is small, make purchasing an elegant chandelier a priority. The wear and tear that the years have taken on this pressed tin is part of what makes it special to Robin. She wouldn't think of restoring it.

How to Use Tin in Unique Ways

Inspiration: The tin itself—and the scraps we had left over after finishing a larger project with tin. One of the challenges we had when remodeling our home was finding switch plate covers that fit our style. So we decided to make our own. They are beautiful and vintage looking, and very much a part of the Magnolia Pearl look. They are also an excellent alternative to the standard plastic ones you find at hardware stores.

A note of caution: Always wear gloves when working with tin. It has very sharp edges!

1. Trace around a standard plastic cover onto your old tin, making sure to carefully line up the light switch opening and screw holes. It helps if you oversize the plate a little bit so that you can contour it to the wall.

2. Use a Dremel tool to cut out the holes first. (A Dremel tool is like a small drill with special attachments for different jobs. You can buy one at hardware stores or craft stores.)

3. Using handheld tin snips, cut out the plate itself. To get rid of sharp edges, simply curl them under with some pliers.

4. To install the cover, just use the old screws from the switch plate cover you are replacing.

Other unique ideas for using tin

Tin is incredibly pliable, so you can form it into shapes as complicated as the amount of work you want to put into the project. Ideas include:

* Use it to patch small holes in floors, walls, or doors. Cut the patch bigger than the hole itself and hammer nails all around the edges. Again, when using cut pieces of tin, be sure to fold the edges under and hammer flat to make a smooth patch.

* Use it for floor molding in place of conventional wood trim.

* Use it to cover seams on carpet walls or on wood floors where sections come together from different directions. It's also great for covering around places where plumbing comes up through the flooring.

* Use it as a kickboard under kitchen cabinets or as a splashguard behind kitchen counters.

When using old tin, it's all about the art. Make your own rules.

One note of caution: If you are using tin that has old paint on it, the paint could contain lead, so take necessary precautions when using it indoors or around food areas. I always seal the tin with a water-based flat polyurethane glaze. I also strongly advise everyone to wear a painter's mask and eye goggles when working with these materials. Safety measures are extremely important, especially with children in the home.

Floors

Wood floors are the most flattering for the Magnolia Pearl style—they add warmth. Inexpensive wood flooring is easy to come by these days, as there are lumber liquidators all over the country. If you are remodeling your home and run out of money for flooring, you can paint the plywood subfloor with exotic designs to look like an Oriental rug or simply paint it a solid color. Try not to worry too much about the results, since plywood floors are usually temporary and can be easily covered with antique rugs. Recycled or salvaged wood is another good option for attractive flooring.

If you have carpet and are sure there are wood floors underneath, you should pull up the carpet. Don't be intimidated by the way people talk about the work necessary to maintain wood floors. You don't have to wax them or polish them all the time, and they aren't harder to keep clean. In fact, for my floors, I just use some Murphy's Oil Soap, a bucket of hot water, and a good, old-fashioned yarn mop. You know, one of the nice things about the Magnolia Pearl style is that you should let things age gracefully. With all the beautiful, old things decorating your home, the floor will look better with a little wear on it.

What should you do if underneath the carpet is a concrete slab? Another good question. Pull up the carpet anyway, and paint or stain the concrete. This, too, is beautiful. It can make a room feel a little cold, but that's okay,

OPPOSITE: Wood floors are the perfect stage for this baroque sofa, which incorporates gold velvet, pink French brocade, and of course, the ever-present lace.

because whether your floor is wood, concrete, or tile—or even if you decide to stick with the carpet—the next layer will consist of lots and lots of rugs.

As many rugs as I have on the floor, you might think, "What difference does it make what kind of floor you have?" Keep in mind that the point of layering is to cover beauty with beauty. You want to make sure that the layers underneath are as beautiful as what gets placed above. You can't go wrong with too many rugs. Remember: More is never enough. None of the rugs in my home match; they are all different colors, styles, and patterns. Be on the lookout for antique Oriental or hand-hooked American rugs, and my favorite—Art Deco Chinese rugs. It's okay if they are tattered and worn; that only adds to their beauty. In addition to giving your home a lot of warmth, layered rugs make standing on the floors more comfortable.

Doors

Solid wood doors make such a huge difference in ambience that you'll wonder why you ever settled for the cheap aluminum or hollow-core doors. After all, doors are welcoming gateways into your home. They should make you feel safe and secure and yet make others feel welcome to come inside.

My doors of choice are antique oak doors with rippled glass windows or rustic, old doors with layers of peeling and chipped paint. As for doorknobs, I just love antique glass, metal, and ceramic varieties. These decorative accessories exemplify the attention to detail so prevalent during the Victorian Age. If you're lucky enough to live in an

Size Matters

When buying an old door, make sure to
have the correct measurements for your
doorframe before you purchase it.

If the door of your dreams is just a little
bit bigger than your frame (but by no more
than an inch or two), go ahead and get it.
It's usually not too difficult to shave a door
down to size. Unfortunately, if your ideal
door is too small, then your only option is
to reframe the doorjamb. This can be done,
but it's a lot more trouble.

For a dramatic finish for your door,
use weathered wood as trim around the
doorframe. If you want, add a Victorian
screen door; it's another way of practicing
the art of layering. You may find old
screen doors with their screens full of
holes. Before you replace them with shiny
new screens, try hand-sewing patches of
vintage screen over the holes using a
needle and thread or very thin wire.

older home already, you probably have solid doors; you can tell by the heaviness of them. Otherwise, you can always buy antique doors at architectural salvage companies, antique fairs, or flea markets. Old doors generally don't cost much more than what you would pay at a hardware store for a new one. If the environment allows, I always prefer that exterior doors be adorned with glass windows. Personally, I love large oval ones, because they let in lots of natural light and allow everyone inside to see the natural beauty outdoors. Also, one of my favorite decorating tricks is to use exterior doors for interior spaces, especially for places that aren't private, like pantries and closets. They add wonderful warmth and make your home even more unique.

Most antique doors will have brass or glass doorknobs, old hardware, and skeleton keys. If these parts were removed, go to an architectural salvage place to find more, and while you're there, don't forget to pick up some old hinges to match. Don't be put off by a door with lots of paint on it. Usually, underneath there is a beautiful antique door. Unless the paint is chipped to perfection, I prefer to take them to a professional furniture restorer to be stripped down to raw wood and glass, and then left in that condition to age gracefully. Don't pass on a door just because the doorknob is on the wrong side. Moving a doorknob is as easy as drilling a couple of holes and patching the original ones with a piece of old tin. Patching with old tin instead of with wood filler is the only way for me. I think it looks nicer, and besides, you can never seem to hide a wood filler patch perfectly.

Old doors have so much more character than brand new ones. The rippled glass inset provides the perfect frame for this vintage lace curtain.

The Art of Lighting

YOU ARE BEAUTIFUL . . . REFLECT THAT.

IT ALL BEGAN WITH A CERAMIC GENIE LAMP—not the "Aladdin" kind of lamp that you rub and make wishes with—this was just an ordinary reading lamp. But in my eleven-year-old eyes, it was beautiful. It had a funky shade with multi-colored tassels and the genie's toes curled up in those pointy little shoes. But best of all . . . his eyes lit up when you plugged him in! And when our eyes met on that hot day at a San Antonio flea market, I knew I had to have him. Unfortunately, I only had a dollar to spend . . . and of course, the lamp cost a princely sum of two dollars. So I begged and pleaded with my little brother to loan me his dollar . . . and finally, he too must have been caught under the genie's spell, because my wish for the lamp was granted.

LEFT: This bronze goddess lamp with a fringed shade casts an evocative glow over the guest bedroom.

OPPOSITE: Why not hang a French hand-painted chandelier in the kitchen?

From that moment on, you could say that I've had an obsession with lighting and its subtle, yet dramatic impact on our everyday lives.

The importance of lighting in the Magnolia Pearl home can't be emphasized enough—and by that I mean both natural and artificial light. John and I designed our home to include windows surrounding the entire house with beautiful, old, rippled glass to let the glorious Texas sunshine in. True, you can't knock holes in every wall to put in a window, but you can do the best with what you've got (and, sometimes, you can knock holes . . .).

Daylight Through Windows

I believe nothing adds charm and character to a home like antique windows. There's just something about the way the world looks through wavy glass. And when you open and close those creaky wood frames, they just feel more substantial than the flimsy aluminum varieties we have today. I mean, you have to admire the craftsmanship and mechanics of old windows. Often, they slide along ropes that are attached to pulleys and weights which actually do most of the work for you. It's ingenious!

So in my own home, I have nothing but antique windows. Of course, very few of them match, but I actually prefer it that way. How boring would it be to have everything look exactly the same? The view is different from every window, and like a painting, I believe each scene deserves its own unique frame.

As for window screens, I agree that they are a very useful and practical consideration for the home. However, I personally don't use them. In my opinion, they prevent

Lighting is every bit as important in the bathroom as in the rest of the house. Lace curtains offer privacy while taking advantage of the natural light and a Victorian floor lamp adds unexpected drama to an often overlooked room.

OPPOSITE: Nothing adds charm and character to a home like antique windows. A cut-velvet valance and a decorative cornice from an old armoire help frame the view.

How to Make Window Treatments

Inspiration: The desire to have a modicum of privacy—but not to shut out the whole world. Regular drapes are too heavy, and I like to let in a lot of natural daylight. This is a nice, inexpensive way to dress windows.

How To: It's doubtful that you will find the same pattern of lace in enough quantity to do all your windows, but who'd want them all to be the same, anyway? Don't be afraid to mix and match different types and patterns of old lace. It'll look great. Good sources of lace include remnants, tablecloths, and piano shawls.

1. Choose fabrics large enough to cover the window and buy the kind of metal curtain rings that have a clip attached (you'll find them at hardware and fabric stores).

2. Cut a piece of sturdy picture-framing wire a few inches longer than the width of your window and drive a screw or nail into the inside frame of the window, one on each side. The height depends on the length of the curtain and how you want it to hang.

3. Secure one end of the wire by wrapping it around a screw or nail. Thread as many rings as you need onto the wire. (For example, I usually clip the rings six inches apart on the panel, so I divide the width of the panel by six to figure out how many rings I need.)

4. Secure the other end of the wire to the screw, pulling it as tight as possible.

5. Clip the lace to the rings about six inches apart. Adjust the clips so that the curtain hangs the way you want.

6. If you'd like, nail up old tiebacks with tassels to swag your curtains back.

If you want a bit more privacy, feel free to add old, tattered, hand-embroidered piano shawls, antique brocade, or velvet drapes, preferably in front of the lace. Almost any vintage textile makes a nice window treatment.

natural light from entering, and thus, darken the entire room. And to me, they're just another unnecessary barrier to the outside world. John and I love to look out our windows and watch the chickens peck or the whitetail deer grazing in the field. You just can't see the same detail and color through a screen. And, yes, when we open the windows, some mosquitoes and flies do find their way inside, but for me, a few bugs are worth the trade-off for an unobstructed view.

Now, antique windows do have one drawback in that they can be somewhat energy inefficient. However, you can reduce this effect with proper insulation of your attic, walls, and floors. In my case, I really don't mind if my own home is a little bit drafty—that's what cozy, crocheted afghans and hot cups of tea are for.

I find antique windows at the places I mentioned in the previous chapter on salvaging—flea markets, antique shows, and stores that specialize in old architectural items. But don't go on your shopping trip expecting to find old windows that will replace what you have as an exact fit. It's just not going to happen. If you find some windows that you love, and they don't happen to fit the exact dimensions of your current windows, it's possible to cut the existing hole a little bigger and frame it in.

The use of earth elements over the windows adds a nice touch. Use flowering vines from the garden such as coral vine (we call it queen's crown or queen's wreath here in Texas) or passionflowers. You could also use hops or

RIGHT: This beautiful piece of vintage lace adds an extra bit of interest to the front door. It's the first thing guests see when they enter the home, and the last thing they see as they're leaving.

grapevine. And keep in mind that you can hang the vines either dried or fresh picked. Of course, fresh vines will dry over time, but they'll become even more beautiful with age. Go a little over-the-top here; don't just hang a little piece of vine up there and be done with it. Really make a statement with it—braid the vines together and swag them over nails hammered into the wall. Embrace your creativity!

Artificial Lighting

Where daylight can't reach, and during the evening and nighttime, you have to rely on artificial light—sconces, chandeliers, and table and floor lamps. Using lots of lights, and in a wide variety, is crucial. All those lights create a subtle mood, casting an amber glow throughout my house that is comforting and soothing.

No matter what you use or where you put it, you need dimmer switches. All those lamps and chandeliers shining at full intensity could make you feel like jumbo jets are landing in your house. So it is essential that every light source be on a dimmer. They are cheap to buy (or you can spend more, if you want to control the mood more minutely) and easy to install.

The bulbs you choose also have a lot to do with the quality of the light. There are several companies reproducing the vintage Edison bulbs, but they can be expensive, so those should be reserved for lamps where the bulbs are clearly visible. For light fixtures in which the bulbs are visible, candelabra bulbs, especially 40-watt bulbs, are another great, economical choice for vintage light fixtures. Obviously, for reading lamps, you'll need a brighter bulb— at least 75 watts.

You can make small spaces in your home feel cozy with the use of little Victorian lamps and chandeliers. Think of ways to alter the lighting sources in places like the laundry room, closets, bathrooms, and hallways. When we were building our house, we installed lights in all the conventional places—over sinks, in the middle of rooms. However, as time passed and we bought more chandeliers, we started hanging them in unconventional places. Now we have a chandelier right over our bed as a reading light, and it's just a few feet away from another beautiful chandelier.

Chandeliers are among the most important elements in my home. If you can't afford a large decorating budget, it's

This hand-painted light fixture is fitted with reproduction bulbs and hangs over the kitchen sink.

OPPOSITE: Multiple light sources, including two chandeliers, provide light for bedtime reading (and plenty of ambience) in the master bedroom.

In addition to the beautiful sunlight streaming though the large windows, three distinctive chandeliers illuminate different areas of the kitchen in the main house.

worth dedicating most of your money to a nice chandelier—it makes such a dramatic statement. Just like anything else, chandeliers can be (very) expensive, but that doesn't mean they all are. Some of our prettiest ones were bought for under a hundred dollars, so don't exclude simple chandeliers just because you can't afford expensive, fancy ones. Or you could get some simple bronze Victorian parlor lights that just need to be rewired—I've seen them for less than fifty bucks. Put several of these around your home, and it'll still be beautiful. Then maybe one day you'll be ready to trade up for that sexy hand-cut crystal chandelier you've had your eye on—never forget about the art of the trade!

Floor lamps, table lamps, and wall sconces are other sources of lighting used throughout our home. Scattered on almost every table, beside every chair, or behind every sofa is a lamp of some sort. Among my favorites are the chipped, ornate alabaster lamps; bronze Victorian lady statue lamps; art nouveau style lamps; and, curiously enough, several lamps depicting the Greek goddess of hunting, Diana.

Wall sconces also figure into the scheme. They are great around a mirror or to highlight art on a wall. Another thing about them is that they can be made from light fixture parts, such as an ornate chandelier arm.

In fact, once you get started, you'll see that you can use old lights in lots of creative ways. For example, I took an old

OPPOSITE, clockwise from top left: No lampshade is ever too tattered to make a design statement. The pressed tin ceiling enhances the beauty of this rescued treasure—not that it needs any help. An alabaster Greek urn lamp purchased from our friend Don Yarton, one of the greatest antique dealers we know. A 100-year-old lampshade hung upside-down shades a Victorian parlor chandelier.

> "A nice chandelier dresses up a room the way an expensive pair of shoes dresses up a simple suit—and like shoes, you can never have too many chandeliers."

bronze lamp that was a statue of a nude woman, hardwired it, and mounted it to the wall in our bathroom. It makes for a striking and unique light source. You could also take an old Victorian or Oriental lampshade and hang it upside down over a chandelier to create another unusual light source.

Don't pass up a chandelier or lamp that you really love just because it needs some TLC or you don't know where to put it. Lamps are simple to repair, and there are companies that reproduce every part of vintage lighting sources. And I often find a place to use a light after I get it home.

No matter how gorgeous your lamps are, they can be ruined by ugly lampshades. An old lamp with a new shade looks scarier than a new lamp with an old one. Finding a vintage lampshade is a real triumph, since they don't tend to last as long as the lamps they came with. My personal favorites are (surprise!) Victorian with fringe, beads, and tassels. They are hard to find in good shape, and they are usually fragile. Yet, even in their aged, tattered condition, they can be more beautiful than something brand, spanking new. They have a comforting appeal, much like your grandmother's old wedding dress.

Other kinds of lampshades to look for are those with metallic lace, long French tassels, hand-painted shades, silk-embroidered Oriental shades, and lace lampshades. Don't forget that tea staining can be a great way to give a new lampshade an aged look.

How to Make a Lampshade
Using an Old Frame

Keep an eye out for old lampshade frames (and save the ones you're left with when the original fabric just becomes too tattered). You can do wonders with vintage lace and fabrics. Here's how I recovered an old lamp shade frame with lace, decorative binding, and fringe.

Setting the Mood with Lighting

According to Taoist philosophy, Yin and Yang are the two cosmic forces which maintain harmony in the universe. The essence of Yin is darkness, while Yang is full of light. Well, I believe the same reasoning can be applied to interior design, because if the Magnolia Pearl style is the Yin, then chandeliers and lamps are the definite Yang. With all the heavy and somewhat dark fabrics typical of the Victorian period, lighting provides the necessary balance for a comfortable, welcoming space. And when it comes to layering, appropriate lighting is crucial, because it illuminates the color, texture, and detail of each individual element.

You know, when I walk through my front yard, I'm greeted with hundreds of twinkling Christmas lights woven through an arbor over the gate. Once inside, the light from crystal chandeliers and Victorian lamps fills the room with a warm, soft glow. Instantly, I feel at home and at peace. There's no way I would experience the same emotions if I walked into a dark, shadowy room or even worse—an ultra-bright space where you're bombarded with the greenish glare of fluorescent lighting and its monotonous hum. I can't imagine anything worse—and neither should you. Make the choice for lighting that enhances your home's ambience and illuminates your life.

The red shade and added fringe make this the perfect boudoir lamp.

The Fearless Use of Color

COLOR IS THE PULSE THAT MAKES THE HEART BEAT.

WHEN I WAS A LITTLE GIRL, my dad and I often walked along the beach. Once I saw a crab claw in the sand and picked it up, captivated by the different shades of red, pink, yellow, and orange. The two of us spent quite a while trying to identify them all. I was impressed by how much detail and color my dad saw in it. I thought all of the different colors were so beautiful that I wanted to keep the crab claw . . . you know, for an art project. When I got home, I decided to tie a string around it and wear it as a necklace.

LEFT: Since childhood, Robin has turned to the colors of nature for inspiration.

OPPOSITE: A kitchen still life, with a bright mix of pottery styles and natural forms highlighting the hand-painted cabinet doors.

Of course this sweet little story could end right there. After all, it's a telling tale of an event that helped to shape and enrich my color palette. But there are more layers.

Now, on any other kid, a crab claw necklace would stand out, but I always had on lucky rabbits' feet, candy necklaces, feather boas, and all kinds of other things. After a couple of weeks of wearing my crab claw necklace to school, a certain . . . aroma . . . filled the classroom, and my teacher soon traced it to me. Thinking that this poor little hippie child was in desperate need of a bath, she sent me home. Well, my parents had been searching for the source of the stink too. They made me strip down to take a bath, so they discovered the crab claw necklace . . . and that was the end of that.

Still, even after the crab claw was thrown out and I was cleaned up and it became another funny family anecdote, the memory of the shimmering colors of that crab claw stayed with me. It helped teach me about Mother Nature's genius, and it still inspires me.

Color is a key element to the art of layering. Try to come up with color combinations that make your heart sing. Unlike me, some people are very concerned with color coordination. For those folks, I would suggest they concentrate on matching hues. For instance, pastels tend to go together. Jewel tones look best with other jewel tones. And a fusion of bright colors can be visually striking. Don't be afraid to experiment. Personally, I find the most inspiration in nature's unbridled use of brilliant colors. My favorite color, for example, is conch shell pink. It reminds me not only of the ocean, but of my Great-Aunt Helen. You see, she loved pink too, and her entire home was filled

with her pretty pink treasures. So today, I associate that color with feelings of warmth and love. You see, when decorating your home, you need to choose colors that don't just look good. They should make you feel good too.

Conch shells add texture and natural beauty to a room, no matter how they are displayed—and conch-shell pink is Robin's favorite color.

OPPOSITE: In Robin's opinion, you can never have too many bird paintings—especially if you have a spacious farm house in which to display them.

In Black and White

I think most people would be surprised to learn that one of my most favorite colors is . . . white. There's just something about it that's very soothing to both the eye and the mind. White spaces have a Zen, meditative quality that I find to be very peaceful and relaxing. I'll confess that I actually tried to create an all-white bedroom once. It was gorgeous--seashells everywhere, vintage lace curtains and coverlets—all in subtle shades of cream, beige, and ivory. It was a monochromatic masterpiece. But I just couldn't help myself. I threw in an emerald green pillow and then a ruby red bedspread. And before I knew it, I was right back where I started. As much as I like white, it's a real challenge to incorporate it into a décor that's rich in jewel tones and bright colors.

On the other hand, I believe the color black fits in quite well with the Magnolia Pearl style. A punch of ebony here and there adds contrast to a room and brings other colors to life. The Victorians actually incorporated quite a bit of black into their decorating, but I wouldn't go overboard with it. I think a dark, black room can be a foreboding, depressing place. So use black, but use it sparingly. A little bit of black adds a touch of sophistication to a colorful room.

There's No Such Thing as Too Much Color

The layered look of Magnolia Pearl is based on a multitude of color combinations.

Don't feel inhibited about using a lot of color. If you find two or three—or ten—colors that you feel look good together, then go for it. When I design something, I try to use as many colors as possible. I admire the Victorian era for its rampant use of color. I had a hundred-year-old piano shawl that was bursting with bold, electric color: vibrant lavenders, ruby red, and cobalt blue. Sometimes I will get inspired from a single piece of fabric and build my designs around that.

It's also important to mix what I call "textured colors." These are things like embossed brocades, embroideries, silks, lace, and velvets. All those textures absorb and reflect light differently. It makes the colors less one-dimensional and more alive, like the pearlescence inside an oyster shell or the wings of a butterfly.

It's important to mix and match textures, patterns, and colors when reupholstering furniture. This Victorian couch frame is covered in vintage silk and hand-embroidered fabrics, and trimmed with Victorian silk lampshade fringe, handmade piano shawl tassel, antique lace, and antique velvet flowers.

"Between my father painting every surface of our home every hue imaginable, and my mother's medley of fabrics, my parents blasted my mind with their psychedelic use of color. In the sixth grade, my art teacher gave me a box of primary-colored paints and challenged me to create as many other hues as possible. That's when I realized how amazing all the colors could be."

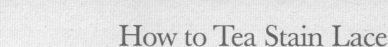

How to Tea Stain Lace

Inspiration: My mother used to do this for her projects, and I remember how beautiful the textiles looked as she pulled them out of the pots of tea. Tea staining adds a patina and makes the palette look richer. Plus, it's completely reversible. If you don't like the results, just soak your fabric in Biz and wash out the stain.

How to: This simple project is recommended if you want to add a quick, rich patina to a fairly small piece of fabric. It's good for staining curtains, cloth lampshades, and tablecloths.

1. Fill a three-gallon pot with water and bring to a boil. The amount of tea you use depends on how much fabric you are dyeing and how dark you want it. For instance, a stain of medium intensity will require about fifty family-sized tea bags.

2. Let the tea steep for about 15 minutes, or until the water is dark. Pull out the tea bags. If you tear a bag, simply strain the tea before adding the fabric.

3. Submerge the fabric and let it soak until the desired shade is reached. Pull it out, but don't rinse it unless you want to lighten it. Keep in mind that the fabric may lighten a bit in color as it dries. If it does, and you prefer a darker shade, then just re-stain it with a more concentrated tea solution.

4. Hang it on a clothesline to dry or put it in the dryer.

Remember, if you have to wash the fabric eventually, the tea will wash out. But that's okay—you can always restain it.

OPPOSITE: Tea-stained lace drying in the Texas sunshine. This effect can be used for materials for curtains, tablecloths, lampshades, bedding—let your imagination be your guide.

A great way to come up with a color scheme for your home is to get out of it. That's right, step out the front door and take a walk through the country or even around your neighborhood. Look around and really take notice of all the beautiful colors in Mother Nature's palette. Find inspiration in the vibrant beauty of bird and butterfly wings. Make a collection of the rocks, sticks, shells, moss, and leaves that you find along the path. When you return home, find a way to incorporate those natural colors into your décor. Bring the spirit of the outdoors indoors and make it a meaningful part your life.

Colors and Moods

As I mentioned before, I do find some colors of the spectrum to be very uplifting and others somewhat depressing. It's natural. I think each one of us is drawn to different qualities of color based on personal proclivities and past experiences. And that's fine; you should surround yourself with colors that speak to you somehow, and for whatever reason, make your spirit soar.

Certainly, do not be ruled by color trends in home décor. Go into any store these days and you see the same colors over and over in everything from wastebaskets to bedding. So-called marketing "experts" come up with these color combinations and tell us that everyone else likes them, so we should, too. Well, I believe that we should make our own rules and following our own instincts. Styles come and go, but interior decorating isn't like fashion. For most of us, it lasts a lot longer than one season. So when decorating your home, choose colors that you can really live with and love.

Don't allow habit to prevent you from experimenting with new colors. It's an easy mistake to make—and I've even done it myself. For instance, I used to steer completely away from the color navy blue, but as I collected more and more Chinese Art Deco rugs, I discovered that it's actually a foundation color for the artwork. Now I love navy blue and I value its contribution to the overall look of my home. So for most of us, color appreciation is always evolving. It's a life-long process that can be personally challenging, but very rewarding, as well.

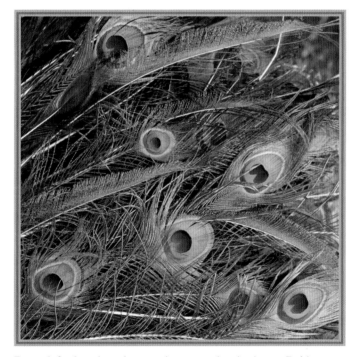

Peacock feathers have been an important inspiration to Robin since her parents became caretakers of a five-hundred-acre ranch—and the four hundred or so peacocks that resided there.

OPPOSITE: Piles of jewel-toned European cut velvet just waiting for their perfect use.

Layering, Room by Room

FOR MOST KIDS, a playhouse is a place to get away from the grown-ups and play "make-believe family" with friends. But as a budding "flower child" in California, naturally, I took an unconventional approach. For me, playhouses were the ultimate art projects—and my first foray into interior design. My father usually helped me build the structure itself—whether it was a treehouse or an A-frame clubhouse in the backyard. We used salvaged materials for the walls, windows, and doors. But then it was up to me to decorate the space to my little heart's desire. By the time I was done, those little

LEFT: Cushions and pillows in Magnolia Pearl furniture are stuffed with goose down to achieve an Old World feel and appeal.

OPPOSITE: Although the dining area in Robin and John's home is relatively small, it still feels grandly elegant and open.

houses were spectacular showplaces with Oriental rugs, antique trunks, a mohair couch, old lamps and even crystal chandeliers. It was my own groovy little retreat from the outside world—the place where I truly learned how to create a comfortable, yet luxurious living space.

As I've said, Magnolia Pearl was born from a salvage mentality, which is essentially being able to discern between treasure and trash and then make something beautiful happen. The art of layering was born out of necessity, because when you are as addicted to beautiful things as I am, your addictions become collections, and you don't want to keep those things hidden away in boxes, so you display them. There's no point in collecting things if you can't show them off, but you don't want your home to look like Sanford and Son's junk shop. (That was one of my favorite shows as a kid, by the way.) You need to find a way to organize and display your things. The more you do it, the more skilled you become at adding more layers. As you now know, layering also applies to the foundational aspects of your home—walls, ceilings, floors, doors, and windows—the parts that make up the actual structure.

You will also want to take into account the purpose of the room you're building foundations for and layering objects into. Certain things work best in the kitchen, say, while others work best in a bedroom. Let me give you a brief walk-through of our home, and you can refer to the pictures to see what I mean.

Step up onto the front porch (watch out for the two guard-turkeys, Leroy and Homer), where there are beautiful Oriental rugs on top of more old rugs covering the wood deck. Several places to sit are scattered around: a Victorian

One of Robin's chickens in a contemplative mood.

OPPOSITE: A Magnolia Pearl fainting sofa adorned with hand-stitched antique crocheted lace and what seemed like miles of painstakingly hand-torn seaweedlike silk fringe. The nineteenth-century painting features Diana, the Greek goddess of hunting.

sofa that has been recovered with big goose-down pillows, an antique porch swing, and a needlepoint covered chair that is frayed in spots. A big wooden table sits behind the sofa, decorated with a pewter vase filled with dried flowers and vines sitting atop a tattered piece of lace and seashells scattered all around. Another table holds a bronze statue and another vase filled with peacock feathers. The exterior wall is covered with old pressed ceiling tin (in fact, the entire house is covered with it). Hanging on the walls, you might see several paintings, more dried vines, a couple of Victorian parlor lights by the front door, and a collection of conch shells tied together, cascading down the wall with their beautiful pink bellies exposed. Looking up, you notice rusty, corrugated roofing tin on the ceiling. Two or three vintage chandeliers hang overhead, and another floor lamp sits nearby with a charming handmade, fringed lampshade on it. Right next to the front door is a plaster statue of a woman, welcoming you into the house. A couple of pieces of tea-stained lace hang in the window of the door.

I'm going to talk about exteriors in Chapter Nine, so I won't say more about that here. But I do want you to notice that, once you're inside our house, that same look you find outside saturates the entire home, only it's magnified. There are dozens of Persian and Oriental rugs on the worn, wooden floor, and there are little cut pieces of tin patching holes in the floor. The house is a sea of lace,

Robin and John's house is a sea of lace, velvet, brocade, tapestries, and fringe—and that look begins outdoors. Here on the front porch, the treasures include beautiful Oriental rugs on top of more old rugs, an all-lace sofa beside an all-lace Mary Poppins bag, and a tapestry and goose-down upholstered ottoman.

velvet, brocade, tapestries, and fringe. There are peacock feathers galore. Seashell-covered boxes hold pieces of vintage jewelry and cameos. Paintings of nudes hang on the walls, and the walls themselves have been painted as though they were covered with antique wallpaper. There are almost twenty chandeliers hanging from the ceiling, in addition to the other dozen lamps scattered around.

While that Magnolia Pearl look fills the whole house, each space is dealt with a little bit differently, according to its purpose. Let's consider them one by one.

Kitchen

In a lot of homes these days, the kitchen feels like a separate entity from the rest of the house. While most of the décor is warm and inviting, the kitchen is a dull, clinical workspace that feels more like a hospital than a home. It seems that somewhere along the way, we began to equate clean with cold, and it simply doesn't have to be that way. I firmly believe that the Magnolia Pearl style fits in as well in the kitchen as any other room.

For instance, in our kitchen, we have vintage rugs on the walls, old lace in the windows and hanging chandeliers— just like everywhere else. And it doesn't look out of place at all, because there's an organic flow from one room to the next. I firmly believe that the very same decorating techniques and attention to detail can be applied throughout the home. You know, we all spend a lot of time in the kitchen, so it should be a place where we feel comfortable, content, and inspired to create artful food.

The Magnolia Pearl style fits in the kitchen as well as any other room. In the main house, a great flea-market painting hangs above Robin's vintage stove. Note the cut-out carpet on the wall, too.

OPPOSITE: In the guest house kitchen, an old refrigerator that Robin bought for thirty dollars at a garage sale is painted conch shell pink. The weathered wood of the island has a new cherry top.

I would suggest that you begin with a foundation of antique cabinetry (available through architectural salvage firms). With their crystal drawer pulls and glassfront doors, they really add a charming touch to the kitchen. I also like to decorate the inside of my cabinets with a little hand-painted feature such as flowers or a pretty design, as a fun surprise for guests when they open the door. In decorating, it's always important to incorporate natural elements, so for your countertops, consider using a material such as stone—especially one that is native to your area. For instance, the countertops in my kitchen are covered with small river rocks that John and I found along the Medina River near our home in the Hill Country. As a meaningful alternative to tile or some artificial substance, these smooth, white rocks are evocative reminders of the beauty outdoors.

In keeping with the Magnolia Pearl style, vintage appliances would obviously be ideal—and old stoves and refrigerators are certainly an option, although the cost of repairs must usually be considered, as well. However, the good news is that, in my experience, those old appliances were built to last. Take for example this old fridge I found at a yard sale for thirty bucks. It was in perfect working condition, but this thing was ugly as sin. Someone had spray-painted it a repulsive chocolate brown on the outside, but on the inside, it was this pretty 1950's-era mint green. No matter what it took to make it presentable, I knew I had to have it. Then, after I got it home, I knew I couldn't just paint it with a brush or something. It needed a seamless

shiny, paint job—like a car! So I took it to a local auto body shop and asked the bewildered, but helpful mechanic to paint my refrigerator-conch shell pink. Today, it's a wonderful, whimsical addition to my sewing studio. Every time I get a bottle of water or a piece of fresh fruit, my retro-refrigerator makes me smile.

At this point, I should note that vintage appliances usually aren't as efficient or easy to use as the modern variety. I learned that lesson the hard way with yet another old refrigerator that required regular defrosting. After a few years of that drudgery, I learned to truly appreciate the

Enhance the foundations of your interior. A wooden column with plaster capital and antique ceiling tin set the stage for a metal fretwork chandelier and hand-crocheted lace.

OPPOSITE: Every nook and cranny of Robin's home is filled with exotic treasures, like this antique bronze angel.

words "frost-free." So if you're a gourmet chef or even a busy mom, you might want to invest in the reproductions that are widely available on-line. They look just like the originals and work with all the convenience we expect today. These reproductions may cost a little more than the mainstream, but the nostalgic atmosphere they bring to your home is priceless.

Dining Room

When we designed our home, it was very important for me that it be a spacious, airy place that was filled with light. So instead of coming up with a layout that divided the house into "rooms," we focused on creating "areas" that flow naturally together. As a result, one of the many unique aspects of our home is the almost complete absence of interior walls and doors. Visualize this: When you walk in the front door, you can pretty much see the entire home living and dining areas, kitchen, office, even back into the bedroom—everything but the bathroom is visible from the point of entry. Now, my home could have ended up looking like some kind of cavernous warehouse or an antique furniture store, but it really doesn't. The trick was finding a subtle way to divide the areas without relying on arbitrary placement of walls . . . which brings me to the discussion of my dining room. It's positioned near the kitchen, but set apart architecturally by old wooden columns with scrolled plaster capitals. I've also hung antique lace curtains from the ceiling to act as delicate, sheer room dividers. Consequently, even though our dining area is somewhat small, it feels grandly elegant, yet cozy all at the same time.

When Robin designs a piece of furniture, she begins by draping fabrics and tapestries over the frame. Here are some prime examples of her work: a carpet-covered ottoman and a Victorian couch covered in French brocade, curtains, and antique cut velvet, accented with hand-embroidered pillows.

OPPOSITE: This old metal lawn chair has been converted into a San Antonio Spurs chair (so-called because John likes to watch basketball games while sitting on it). The fluffy down-filled cushion is covered with French brocade that formerly served as a set of curtains.

As for furnishings, I would begin with an old, sturdy wooden table with leaves that you can add for entertaining. Then using some comfortable, overstuffed chairs for seating. And don't worry about finding a full set of coordinating chairs. Have fun with it! Mix and match colors and textures until you find the perfect combination for the space. Like I always say, no two dinner guests are the same, so why should their chairs be? Throw in an antique rug and top it all off with a lovely chandelier. Remember, in this part of the home, a dimmer switch is essential to create an intimate mood for dining. *Bon appétit!*

Living Room/Den

In my own home, I believe the living room best exemplifies the technique of layering. It is a lush mélange of fabrics, textures, and colors of all kinds. From floor to ceiling, every square inch is covered with layer upon layer of ornamentation and art.

In keeping with the Magnolia Pearl style, the furnishings are primarily Victorian era. However, I've re-upholstered the sofa and wingback chair frames with a hodge-podge of opulent fabrics such as cut velvet, tapestry, lace, needlepoint, silk and satin brocade. The sofa's thick cushions are stuffed with down, making it a "comfy" place for an afternoon nap.

In my opinion, seating arrangement in this area is critical. Although I have a television in the living room, it is by no means the center of attention. In fact, I think the presence of the TV and other modern electronics should be downplayed as much as possible. This enjoyable, but ugly

OPPOSITE: The back porch, resplendent with Magnolia Pearl couch and ottoman, and a faux bois table.

When Robin found this very old dresser at a flea market, the top was destroyed. Covering it with old carpet gave the piece new life. Another rescued treasure: the Texas-style armadillo purse filled with brushes and hand mirrors.

equipment can always be concealed in an antique armoire or hutch. Another option with the flat-screen models is to simply drape a tapestry over it when not in use. Remember, the living room is where you'll do most of your entertaining, so to facilitate conversation, arrange the furniture in a circular pattern. That way your guests can focus on each other (as well as the décor!)

In the center of the room is a short, but large, round table displaying books, mementoes and various works of art. In my experience, it can be difficult to find a so-called "coffee table" that fits in with the rest of the room. So feel free to follow my example and re-purpose an old dining table. When you find one that you like, just cut the legs down to the desired height to accommodate space and function. As I mentioned before, I'm a firm believer that cherished family heirlooms shouldn't be tucked away in a box. They need to be displayed somewhere they can be appreciated and enjoyed—and the living room is the perfect place to do it. Every nook and cranny of my home is filled with exotic treasures like my collection of Majolica pottery, a brilliantly plumed stuffed peacock, and of course, dozens of incredible old statues from around the world. There are Victorian-era bronzes and century-old figures from Japan, as well as alabaster busts of ancient goddesses from Greek and Roman mythology.

It seems that I'm drawn to statuary that features the graceful beauty of the female form, and like a little girl with her dolls, I can't help dressing them up. I adorn my statues with vintage jewelry, rosary beads, crystal necklaces, and pearl collars. I put dried flowers in their hair and crowns of vine on their heads. They hold antique hat pins and wear lace shawls. One brazen lady is nude, so I gave her a fox-fur shrug. Without pants, she may still be a little chilly, but at least her shoulders are warm! Seriously, for me, these "spruced up" statues are a perfect example of the art of layering. Don't be afraid to add your own personal touch to the objects in your home. Decorating is always a work in progress, so embellish, adorn, and beautify the things that truly enhance your life.

Work Spaces

Many people are surprised to learn that the Magnolia Pearl style suits the home office just as well as it does the rest of the home. Although the room may be filled with computers and other modern electronic equipment, it can still be a charming space with nostalgic appeal. Simply let go of your preconceptions about what a workspace should look like . . . and explore the possibilities. I mean, there's no rule that you have to use that dark, boring office furniture. In my workspace, I sit in a French needlepoint chair, while John has a circa-1950's leather chair on wheels. Instead of a desk, our computer and printer are on an old farmhouse table. My paperwork is kept in a vintage filing cabinet with a hooked rug draped over it to soften the edges.

When it comes to accessories, "think outside of the box," and put your ornamental treasures to work in the home office. For instance, I store copy-paper in an antique basket, and pens and pencils are kept in a pewter sugar bowl. For lighting, I use a Victorian lamp that features a statue of a lady beneath a beautiful old shade.

The finished effect is that my home office blends in seamlessly with the rest of my home. I don't feel the need to hide the modern equipment. I simply add decorative touches to make the space warm and comfortable. As a result, it's a place where I feel happy and productive, so I get a lot of work done! My home office is what I call "FUNKtional"— fun, funky, and functional—and yours can be, too!

OPPOSITE: Robin's home office blends in seamlessly with the rest of the house. Although computers and other modern electronic equipment are necessary here, an office can still be a charming space with nostalgic appeal.

Bedrooms

As the place where you begin and end your days, I believe the bedroom has a profound influence on your mood and outlook on life. If you fall asleep in a room that's comfortable and relaxing, and then awake in an environment that's pretty and cheerful, it will undoubtedly brighten your attitude for the rest of the day. Therefore proper lighting in the bedroom is essential. Many people make the mistake of using dark colors on their walls and heavy fabrics for their window treatments in an effort to create a restful space for sleeping. In the process, they turn their bedrooms into depressing caves, which makes it very difficult to "rise and shine" in the morning. The key is finding the right balance with soft, soothing lights and sheer window treatments. Chandeliers and glowing lamps add a warm glow to the boudoir at night, and during the day, multiple layers of crocheted lace will allow plenty of natural light to enter the room.

Bedding should be layered with different fabrics and textures for a soft, luxurious effect. Begin with a fluffy down featherbed and lace dust ruffle. Then create a cozy nest with sheets, blankets, handmade quilts and crocheted coverlets in materials such as brocade, silk, and lace. Top with a generous assortment of pillows in varying sizes and styles. I actually prefer down pillows to polyester fill, because they tend to contour to the neck a little more. Obviously you may not desire as many layers of bedding, in the summertime, so feel free to mix and match according to the season.

OPPOSITE: The bedroom and bath in the guest cottage.

This bed is a study in layering: lace, brocade, linen, ruffles, tassels, and lots of velvet and cut-velvet pillows.

And finally, the most woefully overlooked aspect of bedroom décor—the ceiling. You know, we spend most of our time in this room flat on our backs looking up at it, so we should put as much effort into making the ceiling look good as we do the rest of the room. As I've mentioned you can find old pressed tin at salvage companies and flea markets. Some very good reproductions are also available through on-line suppliers. Other options for ceiling treatments include hand-painted murals and weathered wood boards.

With a little attention to detail, the bedroom can become a peaceful oasis of tranquility within the home—a place to relax, and rejuvenate among the things you love. *Sweet dreams!*

Bath

From what I understand, the hottest trend in bathroom design these days is to install those huge, deep bathtubs with high powered jets spraying water all over your body. I'm sure these indoor hot tubs are nice, but give me an old-fashioned clawfoot tub any day! I've loved them ever since I was a little girl. You see, my grandmother, Helen Brown, had an old cast-iron tub in her home in San Antonio and one of my favorite things to do there was take bubble baths. Being a fun-loving kid, I just couldn't resist sliding down the back of the tub and splashing water all over the bathroom floor. To put it mildly, my grandmother was not amused, but she always managed to smile at my mischief.

Those times in that old tub are still some of my fondest childhood memories. And every time I take a bath in my own clawfoot tub, I feel like that silly, sweet little girl again—and that's a feeling no modern "spa tub" can match.

As the room we escape to for a bubble-bath at the end of a long, hard day, the bathroom should be a calming retreat from the rest of the world. I believe the bathroom should be a place that's comfortable and clean, but not clinical. To me, there's nothing soothing about a stark, white space that looks more like a doctor's office than a powder room.

I think that the bathroom should be furnished as if it were a bedroom or even a small living room. For instance, an overstuffed chair could be placed in a corner to create a cozy little nook for blow-drying your hair or painting your toenails. If space allows, a dressing area should definitely be incorporated into the design of the room. In my bathroom, I have an old oak dresser where I store soaps, lotions, and extra towels. On top are pretty boxes and jars for my jewelry and cosmetics. And instead of an unsightly medicine cabinet, I store all my toiletries inside the dresser drawers. Feel free to experiment with bathroom décor by re-purposing decorative objects in unusual ways. For instance, instead of a tacky plastic wastebasket, use an old umbrella stand or a vintage laundry hamper with a disposable liner.

The proper balance of natural and artificial lighting is also essential in the bathroom. In our country home, privacy isn't usually a factor, so we have several large windows in the bathroom to allow in plenty of sunshine. However, when we do have guests, I simply add some layers of lace to the windows for modesty's sake. Victorian lamps are also a nice touch in the bathroom, providing the soft glow that's perfect for a long soak in the tub.

Fill your bathroom with the things you love. I know that when I'm relaxing in a nice bubble bath, I love to look around at all the little treasures I've collected over the years. It's a time for reflection and meditation. So as a result, my bathroom has become a therapeutic space that genuinely enhances my life.

OPPOSITE: The guest house bath features a salvaged, large, claw-footed tub.

This charming room is filled with many tableaux. Sterling silver brushes, mirrors, and combs, some of Robin's favorite old collectibles, fill an old pitcher. Robin converted the dresser (shown on page 115) into a bathroom cabinet. The small round box in front holds her bobby pins. Robin's great-grandmother kept her bobby pins in it. She passed it to Robin's grandmother, who kept her bobby pins in it, and then she passed it to Robin.

Couture Furniture

> DON'T BE ATTACHED TO THE OPINION
> OF OTHERS . . . IT'S YOUR LIFE. ARE YOU
> DOING THIS FOR YOU OR FOR THEM?

THANKS TO MY MOTHER'S TEXTILE ARTISTRY I gained an appreciation for fabrics at an early age. When we went to the rag factories, my mom told me to stick my arms down in a pile and learn to feel the different fabrics. I felt fur. I felt satin. I felt polyester and cotton and corduroy. After doing that so many times, I learned to discern the difference between cheap rags and quality material. I realized it was just as important to feel texture as to see it.

Most of my fabrics for Magnolia Pearl Couture furniture come from merchants living in France, Italy, Poland, Belgium, and England. These are people who know the quality I demand, and they scout around buying things that would interest me. The rest of the time, I select textiles myself when I am at antique shows.

OPPOSITE: Texture is both a tactile and visual element in Robin's designs. This Magnolia Pearl-Victorian sofa is upholstered with silk velvet, cut-velvet tapestry, French brocade, hand-crocheted lace, hand-embroidered tapestry, handmade lace trim, and Chinese silk embroidery.

Antiques vs. Vintage

You may have noticed that in decorating, terms such as "antique" and "vintage" are often used interchangeably. However, to be precise, clarification is certainly in order, since the exact definitions are quite different. "Antiques" are generally handcrafted objects that are at least one hundred years old, such as furniture, some mechanical objects, and works of art. "Vintage," on the other hand, usually describes items that are not quite as old, but still have a sentimental value, such as toys, collectibles, and appliances, as well as embroidered dish towels and aprons.

As you can imagine, I have a pretty good collection of vintage and antique brocade, velvet, silk, lace, tapestry, needlepoint, and embroidered fabrics, as well as an assortment of tassels, ribbons, and fringe.

> "Go ahead and wash nonwashables—you'll be surprised at the outcome."

If all you can get ahold of is new fabric, it's nice to age it before you use it. To make sure it's going to look the way you want, buy a swatch and take it home. Wash and dry it several times to see how it will look. It doesn't matter what kind of material it is—even velvet—I always wash it to age and distress it. It may shrink, especially if it's high quality, but that's okay. Just be sure to experiment on a swatch to see how much it shrinks so you can plan accordingly. Likewise, if the fabric bleeds or fades, I think that makes it more beautiful. I do tend to stay away from polyester and nylon because they're not really conducive to my style, and it's hard to get an aged look from them. Some fabrics that are generally good candidates for aging include most linens, silks, and rayons.

Old lace and linen tablecloths are another great source of vintage material. They can be easily re-purposed into window treatments, pillowcases, and even clothing. Aprons are another possibility, but in my experience, they're usually made from fabrics that are too frail to re-use.

OPPOSITE: Magnolia Pearl Couture is what Victorian style would have been if Queen Victoria had partied with Janis Joplin and Alice in Wonderland.

It's important to mix textures, patterns, and colors when reupholstering furniture–just let it all hang out. The fabric you use depends on the application. I'll use the more tattered pieces for undertreatments, which include the rear or "outside backs" of the furniture. Obviously, these are areas that don't see as much wear and tear as the seat and back cushions, so the cloth can be a little more delicate. Believe it or not, I sometimes use fabric that is so rotten and worn–but to me still very beautiful–that it would come apart if you pulled on it. This works best on items such as wall treatments or as previously mentioned, the "outside backs" of furniture. The fabric most definitely will need to be replaced when it wears out, but, to me, that's part of the beauty of it. For places that see more abuse, like seat cushions

LEFT: This chair is embellished with tassels, lace, fringe, vintage Belgian cut-velvet, and mohair and accented with an Edwardian hand-beaded pillow.

OPPOSITE: Robin believes the living room best exemplifies the technique of layering in her home. A carpet-covered ottoman and a Victorian couch frame are covered in French brocade curtains and antique cut velvet and accented with hand-embroidered pillows. In fact, every square inch of the room is covered with layer upon layer of ornamentation and art.

Repair, Restore…or Retreat?

When you're in the heat of the moment at an antiques auction or shopping at a busy flea market, deciding whether to buy a tattered old piece of furniture can be a nerve-wracking experience. The typical collector is often unsure if the piece is worth the time, money, and effort that it will take to restore it to the original condition. If you find yourself in this predicament, remember these simple rules:

❋ If it's something that you really love and simply can't live without, buy it. Otherwise, it's not worth the expense.

❋ Don't get it unless it's something you have a place for and can really use.

❋ Don't buy it if there's a good possibility it will end up in your garage or storage unit.

❋ Don't buy it if it means turning your home into a museum where you can "see, but not touch."

❋ Get your priorities straight. You shouldn't become obsessed with the impact a little "wear and tear" has on the piece's market value. You should enjoy the item while you have it.

Note: If you're overly concerned with protecting your investment, these guidelines may not apply. Instead of worrying about profits, I think you should focus on enhancing the beauty and function of the piece. With this mindset, the restoration experience will be much more meaningful and personally rewarding.

and chair backs and arms, use sturdier, heavier fabrics. Things like thick brocades, tapestries, needlepoint, heavy linen, and silk and cut velvets work great for this. The thicker the better, as they need to maintain their structural integrity.

When salvaging furniture to reupholster, look for pieces that are structurally sound. That doesn't mean it can't have some problems—a lot of those can be fixed. Most upholsterers will tighten the frame for you, so don't pass on a piece just because it is loose.

I like to buy old Victorian couches, loveseats, chairs, and ottomans. Whenever I design a piece of furniture—before I take anything apart—I drape fabrics and tapestries over it. Sometimes I will have a piece of textile that I love, and will just start designing around that. Very carefully, I pin, drape, hold, and tuck the fabrics all around in the places and positions where I want them, until I find the best spots for them.

Once I have all the fabrics in place, I make notes and take pictures. Then I send it all to the upholsterer, who takes everything off, strips the furniture down to the frame, and reassembles it according to my design, including always stuffing the seat cushions with goose down.

By the way, it is critical that you find a good, reliable upholsterer—and that's not as easy as it sounds. In my experience, most of them are pretty hung up on traditional rules like keeping the repeating pattern of the fabric consistent throughout the piece, and as you know, I'm not really big on following anyone else's rules. So it is imperative that you find an upholsterer who is flexible, open-minded, and willing to collaborate with you on the project. This person should have excellent craftsmanship skills, since you are entrusting him or her with some fairly valuable materials, so be sure to check their reputation and credentials. Finally, find someone who is creative, cooperative, and willing to take your vision and make it a reality.

I also like to cover dressers and tables with old carpet remnants. It's actually a pretty easy project, and when you are finished, you will have a unique piece of furniture to add to your décor.

This chair is a great example of Magnolia Pearl's couture style: embellished with tassels, lace, fringe, vintage Belgian cut-velvet, and mohair.

How to Make Carpet-Covered Furniture

Inspiration: Necessity—the mother of invention! To see the end result is to love it, because old furniture and old carpet make a perfect marriage. John and I found a dresser with an unsightly top and unattractive drawer facings that was being thrown out. Later on that same day, we came across a couple of beautiful discarded carpets that were rotten on one end. The idea hit me to cover the unsightly parts of the dresser with the attractive pieces of the carpet. It ended up looking so beautiful, we decided to cover the whole thing with the rest of the good pieces of carpet. Whether you decide to cover an entire piece with carpet or just the top, it will have a bohemian feel. This project is good for when the veneer has come off in places, or if you don't want to strip, sand, and refinish a piece of furniture.

How To:

1. With the carpet upside down on the floor, turn the piece of furniture so that whatever part of it you are going to cover is on top of the carpet, and trace the shape of that part with a marker.

2. Cut out the pattern you traced, using a utility knife or heavy-duty scissors; it's best to cut just inside the marker line.

3. Turn the furniture so the part you're going to cover is up and position the cut piece of carpet on it. Attach the carpet to the furniture using small carpet brads or tacks. You need fasteners that will grab into the wood but that are not so big that they'll split it.

4. Using a carpenter's hammer, gently tap the brads through the carpet and into the wood. Apply the brads to one complete side first so that you can pull on the carpet and keep it tight as you go around to finish nailing. I don't worry about a frayed, shaggy edge where the carpet was cut because I like the way it gives the furniture an aged, rustic look. If you want to finish out the cut ends, however, try using upholstery trim, bouillon trim, fringe trim, metal fringe, or antique pieces of lace.

5. Don't forget to replace boring drawer knobs with vintage glass ones or antique drawer pulls. You can even use salvaged doorknobs for this.

Outdoor Living Spaces & Landscaping

LET YOUR INNER EXTROVERT OUT. . . .

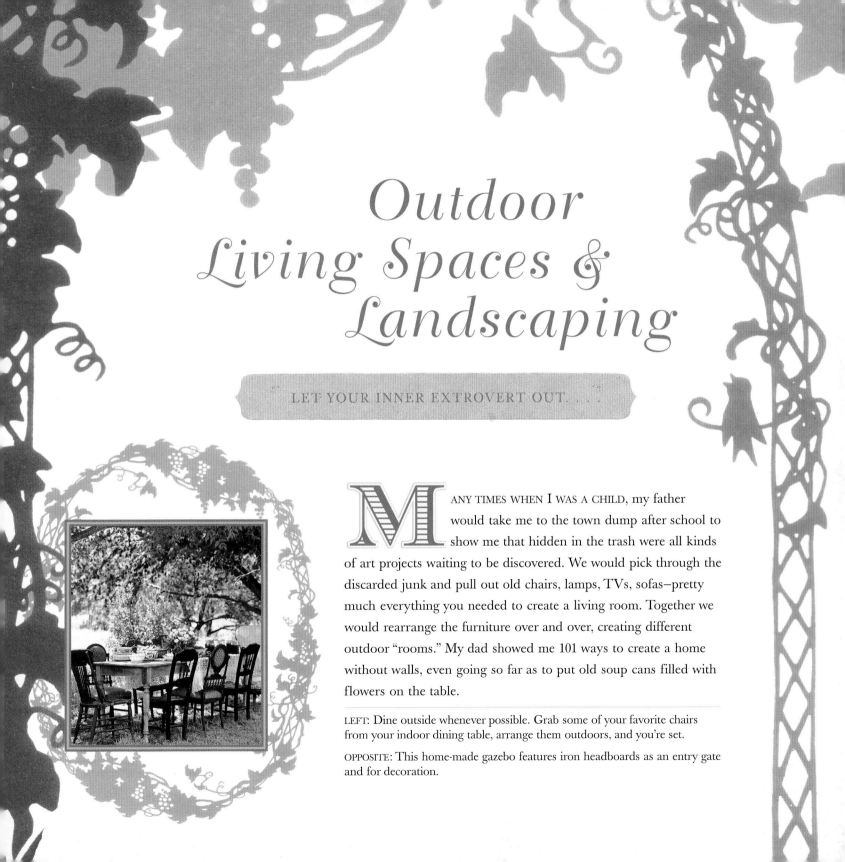

MANY TIMES WHEN I WAS A CHILD, my father would take me to the town dump after school to show me that hidden in the trash were all kinds of art projects waiting to be discovered. We would pick through the discarded junk and pull out old chairs, lamps, TVs, sofas—pretty much everything you needed to create a living room. Together we would rearrange the furniture over and over, creating different outdoor "rooms." My dad showed me 101 ways to create a home without walls, even going so far as to put old soup cans filled with flowers on the table.

LEFT: Dine outside whenever possible. Grab some of your favorite chairs from your indoor dining table, arrange them outdoors, and you're set.

OPPOSITE: This home-made gazebo features iron headboards as an entry gate and for decoration.

I believe this was his way of helping me think outside of the box—because there was no box to begin with! I learned that I could create beauty anywhere—even the city dump.

The exterior spaces of your home give visitors their first impressions about you, and the way you keep them suggests how you keep the rest of your nest. They should be neat, beautiful, comfortable, and inviting—the outdoor spaces should be as lavish as the inside ones. Since John and I spend so much time outside, we put as much thought into decorating our yard as we do the rest of the home.

Porches, outbuildings, animal pens, and outdoor showers (yes . . . outdoor showers) get the same attention to detail as any other interior space in our home. You should feel comfortable using indoor furnishings in outside spaces. Nearly every element you would find inside your home would work beautifully on a big covered porch.

Of course, in many parts of the world, climate and weather conditions can adversely affect outdoor furnishings. For instance, in regions with high humidity, you should consider using fewer exposed fabrics and more moisture resistant substances such as concrete, wood, vines, rocks, and shells. However, in places that are warm and dry much of the year, like the Texas Hill Country, outdoor furniture typically requires minimal maintenance.

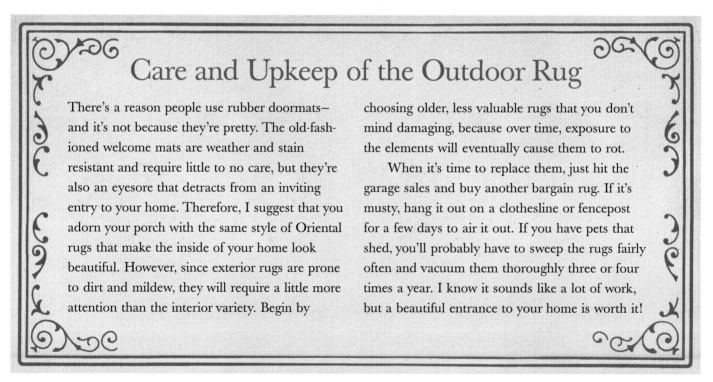

Care and Upkeep of the Outdoor Rug

There's a reason people use rubber doormats—and it's not because they're pretty. The old-fashioned welcome mats are weather and stain resistant and require little to no care, but they're also an eyesore that detracts from an inviting entry to your home. Therefore, I suggest that you adorn your porch with the same style of Oriental rugs that make the inside of your home look beautiful. However, since exterior rugs are prone to dirt and mildew, they will require a little more attention than the interior variety. Begin by choosing older, less valuable rugs that you don't mind damaging, because over time, exposure to the elements will eventually cause them to rot.

When it's time to replace them, just hit the garage sales and buy another bargain rug. If it's musty, hang it out on a clothesline or fencepost for a few days to air it out. If you have pets that shed, you'll probably have to sweep the rugs fairly often and vacuum them thoroughly three or four times a year. I know it sounds like a lot of work, but a beautiful entrance to your home is worth it!

OPPOSITE: Free-ranging chickens meander the garden path.

One is five.
One bunch of bananas. One hand of cards.
One family.

One is six.
One line of laundry. One butterfly's legs.
One family.

One is seven.
One bouquet of blooms. One flock of birds.
One family.

One is eight.
One box of crayons. One row of ducks.
One family.

One is nine.
One flight of stairs. One collection of rocks.
One family.

One is ten.
One batch of cookies. One shelf of books.
One family.

One is one and everyone.
One earth. One world.
One family.

4

5

8

CRAYONS

9

10